T0368073

LOVE GOD,
Love Yourself

143 Encouraging
Devotions While Facing
Life's Hardships and Insecurities

FAITH BOLDE

WESTBOW
PRESS®
A DIVISION OF THOMAS NELSON
& ZONDERVAN

WestBow Press books may be ordered through booksellers or by contacting:

WestBow Press
A Division of Thomas Nelson & Zondervan
1663 Liberty Drive
Bloomington, IN 47403
www.westbowpress.com
844-714-3454

Because of the dynamic nature of the Internet, any web addresses or links contained in this book may have changed since publication and may no longer be valid. The views expressed in this work are solely those of the author and do not necessarily reflect the views of the publisher, and the publisher hereby disclaims any responsibility for them.

Any people depicted in stock imagery provided by Getty Images are models, and such images are being used for illustrative purposes only. Certain stock imagery © Getty Images.

Scripture quotations marked (ESV) are from the ESV® Bible (The Holy Bible, English Standard Version®), copyright © 2001 by Crossway, a publishing ministry of Good News Publishers. Used by permission. All rights reserved.

ISBN: 979-8-3850-4135-0 (sc)
ISBN: 979-8-3850-4136-7 (hc)
ISBN: 979-8-3850-4134-3 (e)

Library of Congress Control Number: 2024927447

Print information available on the last page.

WestBow Press rev. date: 04/29/2025

CONTENTS

INTRODUCTION

Hey y'all, I'm Faith Bolde and above everything else, I see myself as a child of the King. I am forgiven, accepted, valuable, hand-picked, treasured, a citizen of Heaven, and a masterpiece created by God in His own image. However, life can take you down some unpredictable paths where it seems incredibly hard to handle the circumstances you may encounter. This book is intended to showcase some of mine as you turn the pages and discover my successes and triumphs as well as many of my insecurities, doubts, and challenges.

I accepted Christ as my Lord and Savior at an early age having been raised in a Christian home in Santa Clarita, California. Since those early years, I made the decision to give my life to Jesus and was baptized in front of family members and good friends. I have grown in my faith each year and am always looking for ways to glorify the Savior.

I recently graduated from California Baptist University with a bachelor's degree in film production. Additionally, I earned a certification as a wellness coach and walked away with three Division 1 National Championship rings after being recruited as one of the CBU Lancer Dancers. I have danced for over 20 years and am now finding what comes next in my post-college life. It was so easy for me to find my identity in school or dance since both had been part of who I am for as long as I can remember. What I need to stop and remember is that God gave me a number of talents and skills to use. Dance is just one of them. What's important is understanding that those elements of my life are not my identity. They are what I do, but they are not what I am.

I came to realize that in recent years, my identity was stored up in my appearance as a dancer, a model, an actor, and a brand promoter as a social media influencer. With unrealistic beauty standards on social media everywhere one may look, I know many women can relate to the struggle with comparison. News flash, things are edited! Even I have been guilty of airbrushing my skin in pictures. While going through a variety of issues as I was struggling with my own body image and insecurities, I needed encouragement. I had just finished a devotional and started looking for one about beauty aimed specifically toward women dealing with insecurities. The problem was, I couldn't seem to find one.

Who would've thought the girl who never really enjoyed reading for pleasure now wrote a book? I have, however, always loved writing. I looked forward to writing this largely because I have always loved reading daily devotionals in the mornings. I am hoping that others feel the same way about this one.

Through my struggles, I had been writing verses on sticky notes adhering them to my bathroom mirror to look at each day. One day I was reading one and I thought, why don't I just write my own devotional? I started with those verses up on the mirror and created a journal entry that related to each one. The process became therapeutic while I was still dealing with my own insecurities. It was originally written for myself, but as I kept writing, I realized that a lot of what I experienced just might resonate with other girls my age although I believe most women can relate.

I chose 143 journal entries because I had learned that "143" translated into "I love you" when pagers were used before my time. When it is hard to love ourselves or when a relationship ends, a friendship dissolves, or even a family member leaves or dies, it is a direct reminder that God's love for us never ends. Psalm 100:5 says, "His love endures forever." The equivalent would be 1434E. And when you fully understand the love of God, you can love yourself.

A wide variety of topics are shared about my experiences with skin issues, body image, comparison, security in relationships, friendships, and trying to control everything when all I could truly do was surrender all those things to God.

I am certainly not perfect, and I am not a pastor or seminary student, but I felt the Holy Spirit leading me to author this book. Although I still deal with insecurities from time to time, the process of writing this devo has been a part of my healing process. I have learned and grown so much. I pray that these verses and journal writings are not only a reminder to me, but to the reader as well. I pray that you are reminded that you are loved, and insecurities do not define you. God doesn't make mistakes. He made you exactly who you are meant to be. My hope after reading this devotional is that you will be confident in that extraordinary fact.

1

EVERYONE HAS INSECURITIES

"You are altogether beautiful, my love; there is no flaw in you."
Song of Solomon 4:7

One of the main reasons I decided to write this devotional was to not just encourage others but to inspire myself during a very hard time. It may seem vain to some, but unless you have struggled with acne, you don't know how mentally taxing it can be.

Other than the occasional blemish or minor breakout, I was very fortunate that I didn't really struggle with acne too badly in junior high or high school as most do. It wasn't until my last year of college that I began to battle a terrible acne problem. It was officially later diagnosed as "adult female hormonal acne." I will refer to it throughout this book as my hormonal acne. It quickly took a toll on my confidence. I can't even count the number of times I was in my room crying asking, "God, why? Why me? What did I do to deserve this?" Something that took a while for me to understand is that God doesn't always do things for the purpose of punishment; we have a good God who orchestrates everything for a reason.

Sometimes God has us go through things in life to draw us closer to Him or to teach us something. For me, I do not believe it was to punish but to not put so much pressure on myself with how I look. During this time, I wrote down many verses on Post-it notes, which I put on my mirror to look at each day to help encourage me. They reminded me of God's word and helped me see beauty in the day when I couldn't see it in myself. Many of these helpful verses are used throughout this devotional.

As women, just about everyone has something they are insecure about. I encourage you today to write down Song of Solomon 4:7 on a Post-it note and stick it on your mirror to look at whenever you are feeling insecure remembering God made you without flaw.

2
FEARFULLY AND WONDERFULLY MADE

"I praise you, for I am fearfully and wonderfully made."
Psalm 139:14

In this world, we are so quick to compare ourselves to one another, wishing we had what others have. The girl with straight hair wants curly hair and the girl with curly hair wants straight hair. We often want what we don't have. It's important to not let comparison and longing for what we don't have distract us from what we do have with which God has blessed us.

I started dancing at two years old and danced all the way through college where I was blessed to win three Division 1 National Championship rings. I have spent many hours in front of the mirror, and you can pretty much ask any dancer, and they will say at one point or another in their life they struggled with body dysmorphia like, "I wish my legs were skinnier like hers."

When I was in elementary school, I had to do a book report, and I chose the book *Soul Surfer* by Bethany Hamilton. Bethany was only thirteen when she lost her arm due to a shark attack. Whenever I am feeling insecure about my body, I go back to that story and quickly switch my mindset to praising God for what He has given me. I am grateful that I have arms and legs which allow me to move my body and get up and dance.

"Comparison is the thief of all joy," as President Theodore Roosevelt stated. Learn to be secure in yourself, count your blessings, and don't take anything for granted.

Today, instead of standing in front of the mirror and critiquing yourself, I encourage you to name at least one thing you like remembering God made you special as you are uniquely and wonderfully made.

MADE IN HIS IMAGE

"God created man in His own image."
Genesis 1:27

Growing up in Southern California, I have been blessed with many gorgeous sunsets. Each time I see the sky with its incredible colors, I think, how great is our God? He painted that! Well guess what? He also made you…and in His image! If only we could start looking at ourselves the same way we look at sunsets, because He made both. We are just as amazing and just as beautiful.

How awesome is it that God knows exactly how many hairs are on your head? He knew you long before you were even born. God makes no mistakes and does everything intentionally. You are here for a reason, and He has made you exactly as He has designed you to be. It's okay to not be like the others, He has created each person to be unique in their own way. I think it is amazing that the same God who created the mountains, oceans, galaxies, and all the world looked at you and thought the world needed one of you too.

Today, I encourage you to get outside, even if it's just for five minutes. Put down your phone. Remove yourself from any distractions. Spend some time looking around. Take in the sky and the plants all around. You may smell freshly cut grass or hear birds chirping. Let this be a reminder that God has created all of this. He knows exactly how many leaves are on that tree, how many blades of grass are in that yard, and how many stars are in the sky. Except, He cares far more about you because you are designed exactly as He has intended. You were made in His image…be confident in that incredible fact.

4

DON'T STRESS OVER FOOD

"Therefore, I tell you, do not be anxious about your life, what you will eat or what you will drink, nor about your body, what you will put on. Is life not more than food, and the body more than clothing? Look at the birds of the air: they neither sow nor reap nor gather into barns, and yet your heavenly Father feeds them. Are you not of more value than they?"
Matthew 6:25-26

Another thing most women can relate to is restricting themselves from food to achieve a certain look. Doesn't it seem like any guy can shove as much food in their mouth as they want and not gain a pound, and yet us women can simply sniff the food and gain ten pounds?

We tend to put a lot of pressure on ourselves keeping up our physique. Did you know that your body is actually 80% what you eat and only 20% exercise? As an athlete, it was always very important that I fueled my body for as much as I was training. I've mostly tried to eat healthy and have continued to grow my love of nutrition and share it with others; however, I will admit there are times when I would eat "too clean."

Specifically, around the time I was struggling with my female hormonal acne, food became my thoughts every second of the day. "Is this going to cause me to break out?" "Is this going to make me gain weight?" I was avoiding so many foods and constantly wondering what my next meal would be, checking the menus ahead of time to see if there's something I could eat, canceling plans or missing out on opportunities to bond over food like desserts. It was clear that I was struggling with an obsessive-compulsive disorder (OCD) with food as I constantly tried to control what I ate.

It's fine to eat healthily, and of course, it's okay to avoid foods you're sensitive to or allergic to (I've found I'm sensitive to gluten, dairy, and eggs), but there needs to be balance. Also, one's diet should be 80% whole foods and 20% "fun foods." This is something with which I still struggle.

I need to try not to be so disciplined when I become OCD, yet remember when I feel out of control, that I need to remind myself who is… and that is only God.

Before you sit down to eat today, take the time to thank God for providing that meal, regardless of what it may be, and realize that it is nourishment to your body which is God's temple.

5

YOUR AGE DOESN'T DETERMINE YOUR WORTH

"So, we do not lose heart. Though our outer self is wasting away, our inner self is being renewed day by day."
2 Corinthians 4:16

Adults who are older always talk about how they miss their youthful appearance, whether that be their fuller head of hair, the absence of any grey strays, fewer wrinkles, or maybe their teenage body.

As a twenty-two-year-old who had just graduated from college, I was quite the opposite; I wished I looked older. Age is something that became a huge insecurity of mine, which might have stemmed from myself being in a relationship with a guy quite a bit older than me. My parents are thirteen years apart, so the age gap never felt weird, the relationship ended for other reasons. I have always been mature beyond my years, yet I think sometimes people would fail to see what I was capable of at such a young age.

Nowadays, with plastic surgery, Botox, and other procedures, it's ironic that people do it to look younger, whereas I personally think it makes them look older. Many girls my age look thirty because of the work they've had done, leaving me feeling like I look like I'm still in high school. My acne didn't help with this insecurity as that is normally something associated with junior high or high school but can really happen at any age.

Whenever someone would ask what grade I'm in, I would get so offended like, "I just graduated college!" However, I know friends my age who have also been mistaken for being younger, and even one of my past dance coaches, who is thirty years old, is often mistaken for a teenager.

My mom has always told me, one day, you'll be happy if someone thinks you are younger than you really are. Perspective is everything. Enjoy where you're at right now. Age doesn't determine your worth. As we grow older, looks may fade, but inwardly, we are renewed by Jesus.

Whatever age you may be, I encourage you to write down some things that you are proud of that you know now that you did not when you were younger. We are lifelong learners and can always share wisdom with others.

6
WHAT WAS I MADE FOR?

"For we are His workmanship, created in Christ Jesus for good works,
which God prepared beforehand, that we should walk in them."
Ephesians 2:10

In 2023, the new *Barbie* movie came out, directed by Greta Gerwig, starring Margot Robbie as Barbie. Stereotypical Barbie, who is normally deemed as perfect, starts to malfunction, obtaining more human characteristics like cellulite. Because she is a stereotypical Barbie, without her beauty, she starts to question what her purpose is and what she was made for.

This movie was very relatable to me as I grew up dancing at two years old and continued all the way through college. It felt like my identity. After I stopped dancing, I wanted to get into acting, and that industry is highly competitive, and I too felt like I needed to be "Barbie perfect." Around this time, transitioning from dance to acting, I had a lot of stress, which also could've been a contributor to my hormonal acne. Regardless, it made me feel unworthy and made me question what I have to offer besides my beauty, which is basically my resume for any acting or modeling job.

God does nothing without purpose, and maybe He had my face break out to avoid that industry and to teach me that I have so much more to offer than my looks. This devotional certainly wouldn't have been written had I not gone through these challenges. I put a lot of pressure on myself coming out of college with my degree, still not sure what I wanted to do, and I've learned that is okay. Breathe. I find comfort in remembering that God has called us ultimately to share the gospel with others and that is truly what we were made for.

Today, I encourage you to take a pause. Take a breath. Acknowledge what gifts God has given you and think about how you can share those with others.

7

NOBODY NOTICES IT AS MUCH AS YOU

*"Do nothing from selfish ambition or conceit, but in humility
count others more significant than yourselves."*
Philippians 2:3

Being a dancer for pretty much my entire life, I have learned to be a perfectionist and have become my harshest critic. We live in a world where we are constantly focused on ourselves rather than thinking about others. When I was struggling with my hormonal acne, I remember being out in public constantly worrying if people could notice my skin. I was actually really good at covering it with makeup, but you could still see it based on the texture.

At first, I didn't like talking about my acne to anyone, but as time went on, either myself or my mom would address it to friends or family simply seeking advice, and every single person always questioned that I had acne. "Really? I never noticed it. She's so beautiful!" This was always so shocking to me, like how could they not notice? Something I've learned is that literally nobody notices it as much as you, and that can go for any insecurity. Think about how if we saw ourselves the way God sees us, we would never live a single day in insecurity.

Today, go out and remember you are beautiful in God's eyes, and that is all that matters. Don't worry what people think about you; Jesus was perfect, and people still hated Him. Get out of your head! My Aunt always said, "If you're feeling bad about yourself, go help others!" Find a way to help someone today.

8
HE KNOWS MY NAME

*"Beware of practicing your righteousness before other
people in order to be seen by them, for then you will have
no reward from your Father who is in heaven."*
Matthew 6:1

When I was little, I danced a lyrical solo to Francesca Battistelli's song "He Knows My Name." I was never the best dancer, but I was always the hardest worker. I knew I probably wasn't going to win, but I would still do my best to use the gift I was given to honor God.

At the time, I think I somewhat understood the meaning behind this song, but it wasn't until recently, now being much older, that I heard that song come on while listening to The Message, the Christian radio station in my car, and the lyrics hit me. Going from the dance industry to acting, all I wanted to do was get famous. Even in the influencer world, I wanted followers and to be "known." Granted, if I ever got "famous," I would want to use that platform to bring others to Christ. As I was listening to these lyrics, Battistelli sings, "I don't need my name in lights, I'm famous in my Father's eyes. Make no mistake, He knows my name. I'm not living for applause, I'm already so adored. It's all His stage, He knows my name."

Don't do something just because you want to look good doing it or want something out of it like being famous; everything we do on this earth should be done to bring glory and honor to God.

Turn on the Francesca Battistelli "He Knows My Name" song today and listen to it with your eyes closed, envisioning how it may apply to your life.

HEART READY

*"But let your adorning be the hidden person of the
heart with the imperishable beauty of a gentle and quiet
spirit, which in God's sight is very precious."*
1 Peter 3:4

In 2024, Netflix came out with a new documentary, *America's Sweethearts Dallas Cowboys Cheerleaders*. Despite their previous show on EMT, *Dallas Cowboys Cheerleaders Making the Team*, which didn't get the best reputation due to unhealthy body standards, things have changed. In this documentary, coaches Kelly and Judy really push the importance of fueling the girls' bodies, making sure they are healthy (after all, they are athletes), no more weigh-ins or checking body fat, and while there is still a "DCC look," they are embracing "curvier" women now.

This documentary also dives deeper into the personal lives of some of the cheerleaders, including one of my favorites, Reece Weaver. Reece is a phenomenal dancer and absolutely beautiful, but what is even more beautiful about her is her heart. It makes my heart so happy when I see people talking about God on TV and she shares about how she was blessed with her gift of dance and always wants to use it to honor God; and whether she makes the team or not, she knows that God is always in control and has a plan.

As a Christian, some ask Reece her thoughts on the DCC uniform and whether or not it is too revealing. In a podcast with Sadie Robertson, she talks about being the light of this world and not avoiding the darkness. Not to say that the organization of the Dallas Cowboy Cheerleaders is dark by any means, but she says that modesty really is how you carry yourself. You can be doing the same pose as someone else but with different facials and come off completely differently. She also talks about how the uniform is much more than its physical appearance to her. When she puts it on, she sees all the hard work that she put into this journey of becoming part of such a legacy.

A quote that I loved in the show from Coach Kelly Finglass is "don't be too busy getting camera ready that you're not heart ready." Beyond any amount of makeup, the heart is what makes someone the most beautiful.

While getting ready today, think also how you can prepare your heart to go out and help or show kindness to someone today.

10

GOD HEALS

"For I will restore health to you, and your
wounds I will heal, declares the Lord."
Jeremiah 30:17

When I started getting my hormonal acne, I saw a dermatologist and she was very quick to suggest going on Accutane, birth control, Spironolactone, or Doxycycline. I had already used some of these methods in the past and had great skin because of them, but as soon as I came off a medication, my skin would negatively react again because those were only putting a "Band-Aid" on the root cause.

I have learned that acne is an inflammatory condition and is a representation of what is going on internally. I spent a year trying to heal holistically through countless amounts of supplements, hair and saliva testing, extensive bloodwork, a strict diet and lifestyle, expensive skincare, and seeing an esthetician. There was definitely progress, but still nowhere near where I needed my skin to be; not to mention this way of healing was much more expensive than just taking a medication that is pretty much guaranteed to work. When trying to heal holistically, a lot of trial and error must take place for results to show. In addition, I developed a lot of OCD tendencies while trying to create a perfect lifestyle.

Whether a western medicine approach or a holistic route is chosen, it's important to note that healing takes time, and one must lean on God during this unknown time. Trust His timing. Remember that He is the ultimate healer, and He has the power to heal or not to heal.

Prayer is the best medicine. Whatever you may be going through whether physically or emotionally, pray and give it to God, trusting He has the best for you. Have faith that His timing and His plan for your life are perfect.

11

AT LEAST SHE'S PRETTY

*"Charm is deceitful, and beauty is vain, but a woman
who fears the Lord is to be praised."*
Proverbs 31:30

When I was in high school, I was very diligent and worked hard for my A and B grades. It might not have come as easy to me as it did to others, but I made it happen. I was rather sheltered and wasn't the most "street smart" and would sometimes say some ditsy things here and there. I would often receive comments like, "Aww, it's a good thing you're pretty." This statement is shocking to me because I didn't feel very attractive in high school. I don't believe that I had a "glow up" until long after high school when I started to figure out what worked for me regarding fashion and makeup. These comments made me feel like maybe it was more important to be beautiful than intelligent and that is all I could offer, which led to myself doubting how smart I was or ever could be.

Years later, to the girl who struggled back then in science, I finally get it now. You learn better when things interest you or apply to you. I saw that when I was trying to get to the root cause of my acne. I learned a lot about women's hormones, gut health, liver health, ingredients in foods, etc. I finally felt like I was actually smart and wanted to use my knowledge to help others. As a result, I helped my grandpa lose 40 pounds through nutrition, exercise, and lifestyle changes!

Even though healing my acne holistically didn't go as well as I had hoped, I gave it a year and learned so much! I learned to really advocate for myself during this time. I also learned not to put so much pressure on my appearance. I learned many healthy habits that I can take with me while choosing a western medicine approach. It doesn't have to be one or the other or all or nothing. Even though western medicine can be a "Band-Aid" approach, sometimes the best decision is what's best for one's mental health as healing holistically can be draining. I realize that it wasn't a waste. I am grateful for the knowledge I obtained from that time.

Life is so much more than just being pretty. It is much more than striving to be the smartest student in the class. A woman's goal should be to desire to spend every day trying to set a Christ-like example for others and honoring Him in all her actions and deeds.

Can you think of any situations in your life that may not have gone the way you had hoped, but you came out of it learning more or growing stronger? God uses all our life experiences for His good.

GOD PROVIDES

"And my God will supply every need of yours according
to his riches in glory in Christ Jesus."
Philippians 4:19

While healing my hormonal acne, I learned that a holistic approach is extremely expensive. I am so grateful not only to my parents for being supportive and helping me pay for everything financially, but ultimately, it was God who provided.

Looking back, it's hard for me not to feel like it was all a waste of money as it did work to some extent, and may have healed me all the way had I given it enough time, but the lifestyle led to OCD tendencies between having the perfect skincare regimen, eating all organic, taking the supplements, specific workouts, not to mention the expensive lab testing and esthetician appointments. Regardless, God provided. For that, I am grateful. I recognize that some don't even have that option and had to just resort to a "Band-Aid" approach being prescribed a medication.

At the time, I had said that if I ever get famous and have lots of money, I would love to start a foundation for people who have acne and are unable to afford treatments, as I know how mentally taxing it is. It's more than just being vain in the sense of beauty; it's a health issue. Only God knows how much I had cried during that time. Often our plans aren't always God's plans. I am still grateful for all that I have learned through those hard times of trying to heal my acne holistically. Ultimately, I have become more empathetic and want to help others just like God has helped me. God has us go through trials to build our testimony. I like the saying, "If there is no test, there is no testimony." It is important to remember that God does everything for a purpose.

Take a second to look around you today to acknowledge all you have been blessed with and thank God for providing.

13

IMPERFECT BEINGS

*"Not that we dare to classify or compare ourselves with some
of those who are commending themselves. But when they
measure themselves by one another and compare themselves
with one another, they are without understanding."*
2 Corinthians 10:12

With social media, we often see certain celebrities and we put them on pedestals and assume that they have the "perfect life." I understand that there has been a lot of controversy over some of the most famous people in the world, the Kardashians, for example. I didn't watch their show when it first came out. I have since seen a few episodes here and there and it seems as though they may have grown and matured learning from past mistakes. I see them praying, talking about God, and I love how open they are about how their lives aren't perfect. I know they get criticized a lot, but it seems that they really do work for what they've accomplished although their lives are certainly atypical. Regardless, they are human and have insecurities just like anyone else.

I love how open Khloe has been about her weight loss and how she grew up being called the "bigger Kardashian" which I am certain wasn't easy. Kim has also talked about her struggle with psoriasis. Kourtney, the oldest Kardashian, has embraced the beauty in how a woman's body changes whether that be in pregnancy or simply getting older. Kendall struggled with acne. As a model, she was very insecure! Kendall would ask her sister Kylie every day on the way to school if she could see her acne, and every single time, Kylie said "No, you look beautiful." Kendall knew it was a lie, but appreciated how sweet her sister was trying to make her feel better. One of Kendall's top ways of stopping this insecurity was by finding a picture from her youth and putting it on her mirror to look at every day. She would picture herself saying any self-deprecating words to that little girl. By doing so, she would catch herself and stop that negativity. She knew that she would never say those negative words to a little kid, her mom, or a friend, so why would she say them to herself?

We are all imperfect human beings, even when it appears that someone has it all together. Remember, it is very easy to edit pictures, and many succumb to plastic surgery. Don't compare yourself to others. It is important to be content with what God has blessed you with. Only God is perfect.

Today, I encourage you to take a fast from social media to avoid comparing yourself to others. Be kind to yourself with the words you speak to yourself. If desired, try the Kendall Jenner trick. Place a favorite picture from your youth and put it on your mirror.

A HAPPY HEART

"A glad heart makes a cheerful face, but by
sorrow of heart the spirit is crushed."
Proverbs 15:13

Sometimes I look back at pictures of myself when I was "bigger" and feel embarrassed for that past version of me and yet question how I was so happy. I have since understood the benefits and connections of exercise and nutrition. I am fitter now and have had somewhat of a "glow up," yet have never felt more insecure or critical of myself.

Even recently, there are pictures I'll look back on where I absolutely love how my body looks, but at the same time, have never been so insecure about my skin due to my hormonal acne.

I've learned there is always going to be something that makes you feel insecure. As soon as one thing is "fixed," there's another thing you'll find by picking yourself apart. That's why it's important to remember that your happiness shouldn't be determined by your appearance. I know it sounds silly, but I have had many days where I am in a bad mood simply because I didn't like how either my hair or makeup turned out that day.

Remember that true joy can only be found in the Lord, not in your appearance. Go about today being glad God has made you exactly the way you are while acknowledging your blessings. You are unique and special. God made you perfectly and no one else is exactly like you.

Even if you don't feel like it, I encourage you to smile today for just a few seconds. I know it may sound silly, but your mind will be tricked into thinking that you are in a good mood which can quickly change a day around.

15

EXPECTATION VS REALITY

"If I must boast, I will boast of the things that show my weakness."
2 Corinthians 11:30

On social media, I think we often forget that people only post their highlights, the things they want people to see, not showing the hard times. I started to realize this when either mine or my mom's friends who followed me would approach one of us and communicate how amazing it seems like my life is going and how I look like I'm just thriving. Little did they know how much I was crying behind the screen, going through a lot of trials, being tested in so many ways.

There were times when even I would look at my social media and want to jump in being that girl; a girl who seemed to have the perfect life and everything together. Yet, that's not reality. I laugh specifically at a trip I took to the South wanting to portray a southern country girl Pinterest aesthetic. I quickly realized that I hate bugs and despise getting dirty. Clearly it wasn't as glamorous as the pictures seemed, that's for sure! I also felt guilty for smoothing my skin covering up my acne in pictures. I know others viewed my post thinking I had flawless skin, yet they had no idea how much I had been struggling.

Not everything is always as it seems. That's why when I see an influencer being open about their insecurities, I think it is so commendable and encouraging to their followers. One of the influencers that helped me the most while dealing with my hormonal acne was Alix Earle. Having a similar challenge herself, she remembers a time when she felt guilty for posting pictures with altered smooth skin where nobody knew what she was really going through. However, one day she just decided to be open about it and received such positive feedback. As a result, she gained trust and became a relatable influencer. She continues to remind people that it's a normal occurrence and something many go through. It shouldn't deter anyone from going on and living life. She also reminds us that people generally don't even notice as much as one would think. Regardless, God made us all beautiful.

I often like to post encouraging verses or quotes on my Instagram stories, and I truly believe God orchestrates all things for a reason. Looking back at my many trials, I now see that He has helped me through each and every one. I should be boasting about that! I should be authentic and embrace what is real, and not pretend to be a perfect someone else.

Think about what weaknesses or insecurities you may have that God has helped you with and share that with others.

GODFIDENCE

"Therefore, do not throw away your confidence,
which has a great reward."
Hebrews 10:35

I grew up being quite confident in myself. I was fortunate to have this gift of confidence at a very early age. I was the kid who wore three tutus stacked on top of one another and a tiara to elementary school. Even in junior high and high school, I was very confident in who I was. I know it may seem sad, but I look back on some of those times and question why was I so confident? It is embarrassing to admit, but part of me now believes that I didn't deserve to act that way because I wasn't pretty enough then.

When I go down that rabbit hole, I remind myself that every kid has an awkward stage, and I'm grateful to my mom for letting me feel confident rather than tearing me down. Especially in those pivotal years, she knew it was important that her child/ teenager grew up being secure in herself.

It's out of the ordinary that my insecurities didn't start until college and even after graduating. However, I'm glad that I am at a more mature age now to understand that looks aren't everything. Beauty is nothing without confidence. You could be the most beautiful person yet appear unattractive if confidence is lacking. The most attractive quality someone can have is to be confident and secure in who they are. Ultimately, I get my confidence from God. I know that I am a daughter of the King, made exactly as He intended.

Some of my tips regarding how to appear more confident even when you don't feel like it is to keep that chin up so the crown doesn't fall. Walk with a purpose. Look at people and smile. Go about your day practicing these tips and remembering who you belong to as you are a daughter of the King.

GOD'S PERFECT TIMING

"For I know the plans I have for you, declares the Lord, plans for welfare and not for evil, to give you a future and a hope."
Jeremiah 29:11

There are many times when I have been amidst trials and wondering, "God, why is this happening to me?" In the moment, it may be difficult to understand what He is doing, but His plan and His timing are always perfect.

When I encounter trials, I like to try and count my blessings. In my last year of college and when I graduated, I was struggling with acne, and it was mentally taxing. I look back and am thankful that it happened last year when I had stopped dancing to focus on acting, before my skin was breaking out. Ironically, I made this decision prior to the 2023 actors' and writers' strikes, which shut down the industry completely keeping me from my Hollywood pursuit. As luck would have it, all my classes also ended up being only two days each week. I made the easy decision to commute from home forgoing living in the dorms.

Although my skin was breaking out, I didn't have to deal with roommates seeing me put makeup on just to then sweat it off as I danced. During this time, I also realized that perhaps the acting industry wasn't for me as I put so much pressure on myself to have my skin just right so that by the time the strike was over, I could act again. Sometimes, God protects us from situations that we don't even know exist. I know it is important to remember that we have a good God who has a perfect plan, and His timing is always perfect for each one of us.

Whatever storm you may be going through right now, I encourage you to write down 5 blessings in your life. Throughout the day, reflect on those blessings and give God praise for how He continues to be faithful even when being faced with various hardships.

18
JEALOUSY

*"For where jealousy and selfish ambition exist, there
will be disorder and every vile practice."*
James 3:16

I consider myself fortunate never having dealt with bullying growing up. It wasn't until college that I dealt with a lot of drama. Odd right? You would think that people would have matured by then. What was especially odd was I had to deal with several situations where my roommates were much older than me. One strange scenario involved senior girls making me feel unwelcome hoping I would move out before I even moved in. Another circumstance found me amid several girls who absolutely hated me. I was nothing but nice to all of them but the only thing I could come up with was that they had already been friends, and I was the new one in the group. I really had no idea. Still another situation involved a guy and, well, whenever a guy is involved…ha I think you get the picture. Whatever the case may be, girls can be jealous, overly protective, and sometimes just brats.

Some were nicer than others, but some blocked me on social media, called me derogatory names, and laughed at me… I won't get into the rest. The thing that bugged me the most was the fact that these girls acted completely differently when they weren't around me.

While being bullied, I stood up for myself while "killing them with kindness" as I had been taught from my youth. My parents instilled in me that it is important to remember that when someone may not like you, it's probably because they are either jealous, have their own insecurities, or have their own personal issues happening revealing the root of their actions. I have never been that type of person to initiate drama, and sadly I dealt with a lot in college. With that said, I am glad to have experienced it later in life where I am a little bit wiser versus being younger and really letting their comments get to me where they could have hurt me and could have even destroyed my self-esteem. I thank God all the time for His protection and for His infinite grace.

Our job as Christians is to reflect Christ in our daily lives, even when it comes to dealing with those who are hard to love. How can you show kindness to someone you may not get along with or who you might find hard to love? There is only one answer and as difficult as it may be, you need to give the situation to God and start praying for them.

19

TEARS ARE PRAYERS TOO

"I have heard your prayer; I have seen your tears. Behold, I will heal you."
2 Kings 20:5

I can't even count the number of times I have cried this past year struggling with acne. I like to be in control of what I can, and no amount of skincare, facials, eating ridiculously clean, or supplements were working. I was at my wit's end and needed to realize that when things were out of my control, God had it under control. I needed to surrender it to Him and have patience.

I can't even remember the last time I said a prayer that didn't mention the healing of my skin. Sometimes, I didn't even have the words for prayer. I had exhausted all my options of trying to achieve clear skin and had no idea what to do but just cry. Well, guess what? Tears are prayers too. God knows your heart and knows exactly what you are going through. He knows what you are going to pray about before you even say the words.

Sometimes, you just need a good cry to let it all out. A lot of people, especially men, feel the need to be tough and hold their emotions in, but crying will release oxytocin, easing any physical or emotional pain. Whatever you may be going through, remember God sees every tear, hears every prayer. He may heal you or give you the strength and perseverance to get you through your situation or trial.

Whatever trial you may be going through right now, come to God in prayer, asking Him to help you, and if you can't find the right words and start to cry, that's perfectly fine. He knows.

20

THIS TOO SHALL PASS

"For this light momentary affliction is preparing for us an eternal weight of glory beyond all comparison, as we look not to the things that are seen but to the things that are unseen. For the things that are seen are transient, but the things that are unseen are eternal."
2 Corinthians 4: 17-18

When I was struggling with my skin issues, it honestly felt like the end of the world. I was convinced that I'd just never have a clear complexion, and this was going to last forever. However, God promises that this, too, shall pass. We are comforted in 1 Peter 5:10, "And after you have suffered a little while, the God of all grace, who has called you to His eternal glory in Christ, will Himself restore, confirm, strengthen, and establish you." We all go through seasons of life; some harder than others, but it's called a season for a reason. It doesn't last forever.

I had to realize that my acne was temporary and that it wouldn't last forever. God would heal me, eventually. If you could see your life on a timeline, you would also realize that this difficult season of your life is so small compared to the rest, and even more so, our life on earth is so small compared to our eternity in heaven. We literally live on a floating rock. Am I really going to let the state of my skin have that big of an impact on my life? No. Well, I know that is easier said than done, but having this perspective reminds me of what's truly important. I need to remember not to focus only on the things of this earth. I need to think about where my eternity lies.

Close your eyes and give God all your cares and worries. Picture a rope representing the timeline of your life. Make a mark on it. Realize that small mark is your life on earth while the entire rope represents your entirety in heaven. This change gives perspective, doesn't it?

21
THERE'S ONLY ONE JUDGE

"Do not speak evil against one another, brothers. The one who speaks against a brother or judges his brother, speaks evil against the law and judges the law. But if you judge the law, you are not a doer of the law but a judge. There is only one lawgiver and judge, he who is able to save and to destroy. But who are you to judge your neighbor?"
James 4:11-12

When I was struggling with my hormonal acne, I was actually pretty good at covering it up with makeup. However, the texture of my skin could still be seen. Yet even though my makeup was non-comedogenic (doesn't clog pores), I still felt like each time I put it on it was making my skin worse. Not to mention, it took me so long to get ready! Generally, one puts makeup on to feel extra beautiful. I felt the opposite as I was so discouraged seeing the texture of my skin after applying makeup.

For the people who have acne and could go out with no makeup, props to you. I, unfortunately, wasn't that confident. Since my acne was hormonal, it was only on the lower region of my face. Many times, when I didn't want to wear makeup, I would wear a mask to class and lie, saying I was sick. If I was driving with someone, I would ride in the backseat with tinted windows. I would stay home a lot, cancel plans, and the list goes on. I felt ashamed of my acne and did everything in my power to not be seen because I was afraid of people judging me. I wasn't myself at all.

Well, guess what? We only have one judge and that is our Heavenly Father. Anyone else who may be judging you is sinning. Matthew 7:1-2 says, *"Judge not, that you be not judged. For with the judgement you pronounce you will be judged, and with the measure you use it will be measured to you."* Everyone will be judged by the Father one day. We are called to not judge others, and the only person we should really care about what they think of us is God.

Today, I encourage you to go outside. Go on a walk, spend time with family or friends. Stop hiding because of whatever insecurity you may be facing. Realize that most people are so self-centered they probably won't even notice your imperfections anyway.

22

IMPRESSIONABLE LITTLE GIRLS

*"Train up a child in the way [she] should go; even
when [she] is old [she] will not depart from it."*
Proverbs 22:6

Something I have learned as I have gotten older is that insecurity doesn't go away at a certain age. I remember being young and hearing my dad talk about him needing to drop a few pounds. Even today, my mom will sometimes ask me if the dress she is wearing makes her look "fat." She never looks fat; she always looks beautiful. However, my point is this, even adults struggle with their image.

Children are very impressionable. My parents aren't perfect, but I would say that they did a pretty good job raising me into the woman I am today. Especially my mom; she was, for the most part, always very careful what she said around me regarding beauty. Some moms may look at themselves, commenting on their appearance, saying things like, "I'm so ugly" or "I need to lose weight" or even "I'm so fat." In the eyes of any little girl looking up to her mother thinking she is so beautiful, she will hear these words and start to think "Maybe I need to lose weight too," or "Maybe I'm not pretty enough." Even if you aren't saying things directly toward your children, they still listen to what you tell yourself. So, it's important to set a good example. Simply switching the words from "I put makeup on to be pretty" to "I put makeup on to be extra fancy" shows your child that you don't need makeup to be beautiful.

Even beyond all these comments concerning beauty, the ultimate way to raise a child is to teach about God and what is shared in the Bible so that these truths are impressed upon them through adulthood. 1 Peter 3:3-4 says, *"Your beauty should not come from outward adornments, such as braided hair and the wearing of gold jewelry and fine clothes* (I'll add makeup here). *Instead, it should be that of your inner self, the unfading beauty of a gentle and quiet spirit, which is of great worth in God's sight."*

If you have children, reflect on how you speak to yourself in front of them and what kind of impression you may be leaving on them. If you do not have kids, reflect on what you are saying to yourself, whether out loud or internally, and how you can change any negative thoughts as you may have kids one day and you do not want to project negative impressions on them.

23

A BEAUTIFUL HEART

"For the Lord sees not as man sees: man looks on the outward appearance, but the Lord looks on the heart."
1 Samuel 16:7

I believe God has us go through relationships to teach us lessons about what we want, or what we don't want in a future partner. In a previous relationship, neither of us were perfect. I learned a lot and found out many things I didn't know about myself. I also came to realize what mattered and what didn't matter to me in a partner. Although the relationship ended, I discovered one of the things I wanted from a future partner was how he always made me feel beautiful, even when I was at my lowest and feeling the most insecure.

We had been together for a while, and he had seen me with glowing flawless skin and when I was struggling with my hormonal acne. Empathy is everything. He really understood what I was going through as he could relate remembering being bullied in high school for having acne. Even though I'm grateful my skin issues occurred after college, I still associate acne with youth, and this made me feel even more insecure about our age difference.

It is said that God's timing is always perfect, I believe that is true. It just so happened that when I was struggling with my skin, he was also struggling with his own insecurity even though I hadn't even noticed. He decided to do something about it, but there was a waiting period involved with his chosen procedure. During that time, we both loved each other regardless of our insecurities and what we looked like because we knew it was the heart that mattered most, and that's how any relationship should be. Looks will fade as you get older, but the heart stays. It is important to find someone who looks at you for your heart, just like God does.

If you are married, give your partner a compliment. Remember to end by telling them something you love about their heart. If you are dating or in a relationship, think about the future when they are old and grey. Will you still love them? Or are you just enticed by their looks right now? And if you're single, reflect on what makes your heart beautiful to a potential partner.

24

IT'S OKAY TO TAKE A BREAK

"And on the seventh day, God finished His work that He had done, and
He rested on the seventh day from all His work that He had done."
Genesis 2:2-3

Something I have really struggled with recently has been obsessive-compulsive disorder (OCD). I realized that when my life feels out of control, I try to control what I can. However, I try to control a lot! Whether it be organizing, having the perfect workout schedule, eating a diet of all whole foods, getting my eight hours of sleep every night, morning and night routines, the list goes on and on as I try to gain control of something. These are all great habits to have in life, don't get me wrong, but it becomes a problem when I get anxious if I get out of a routine. For me, this anxious feeling generally happens when I am traveling; workouts aren't the same, I never know what food will be available (I try to bring what I can), less sleep, etc.

For my 22nd Birthday, I went to Mammoth Mountain in northern California to go skiing and enjoy the snow. I had not skied in eight years. During both high school and college, our dance competition season was always right around the time of ski/snowboard season, and I couldn't afford to take any chances of getting hurt. I was finally in my post-dance phase of my life and was able to go skiing! It was just like riding a bike and I picked it up rather easily to the point where I had done something I had never done before...I skied down from the very top of the mountain! It was scary, but I made it down safely. It wasn't until the last run of the day that I did an intermediate run and hit a patch of ice and lost control. I went flying down the mountain. I must admit, I'm pretty good at maneuvering but I'm not the best at stopping. I fell pretty hard and in the process, I felt a pop in my knee and knew I wasn't getting up anytime soon. I was rescued and taken down the mountain by the ski patrol. They took me to the on-site medical center. Later, I got an MRI done and it turned out that I had torn my ACL. This was the first big injury of my life. Before that, I had only sprained my ankle once and had to wear a boot for about a week.

This was devastating news, as I knew I would have to rest my leg for quite a while. I still did what I could to train my upper body, but I couldn't train my legs or even go on walks and get my steps in for the day. My OCD was through the roof not having my normal workout schedule, but I learned during this time it's okay to rest! It's not the end of the world. Three months later, by God's grace, my orthopedist said I didn't need surgery, and with all the physical therapy, my leg kind of worked itself out and I'm back and better than ever. Sometimes God has us go through hardships to teach us something. For me, that was to learn to rest, and when you feel out of control, remember who is always in control.

If you are sick, injured, or simply just having a bad day, remember it is okay to rest, after all, God did.

COMPLIMENTS

"Do not let your adorning be external- the braiding of hair and the putting on of gold jewelry, or the clothing you wear."
1 Peter 3:3

Everyone wants to be complimented; I mean, who doesn't? I remember when I was feeling insecure about my hormonal acne issue, I would show up to my college classes having my friends say how beautiful I looked, yet I didn't feel it. On another day when I was feeling really insecure, I had to run some errands and go to four different places, and I kid you not at each place, someone complimented me. I saw this saying that said, "butterflies can't see their own wings," which made me realize, sometimes we can't see our own beauty or qualities that we have to offer. If only we could view ourselves the way others did, or more importantly, the way God does.

When I got those compliments, it brightened my day and made me feel more confident despite my insecurity. My number one love language has always been words of affirmation. This is fine, but what means more, being told you're beautiful physically or you have a beautiful heart? Is your confidence coming from yourself or from other's opinions of you? And within yourself, are you more confident based on how you look, or the type of person you know you are? The heart is truly what God is after in each one of us. I'll leave you with this verse to ponder; Proverbs 27:19 says, *"As water reflects the face, so one's life reflects the heart."*

Get out your journal and take some time to reflect on those last few questions I gave you today.

26
ONE DAY AT A TIME

*"Therefore, do not be anxious about tomorrow, for tomorrow will
be anxious for itself. Sufficient for the day is its own trouble."*
Matthew 6:34

When my skin was breaking out, I hated how it was out of my control because it was hormonal, and I had no idea when it would flare up or calm down. For this reason, I was always hesitant to commit to future plans fearing how my skin might be during that upcoming event or activity.

Have you ever wanted God to just come sit down at the table with you and say "Ok, this is what we're going to do," and then give you a plan? That was exactly how I felt while struggling with my acne. It wasn't that I didn't trust God with my future, I just wanted to know the plan. As a very scheduled person, I love plans, and they are very easy to follow and encouraging when you know they will work. My problem was that a lot of my plans had an unknown factor of whether or not it would clear my skin or whether that be the skincare I was using, the supplements, medication, etc. One thing that I've realized is whatever method I chose; it still took patience, and I needed to trust God's timing. Don't be so focused on how things will look tomorrow, just do what you can today.

Even beyond my skin issues, there was so much unknown in my life after graduating from college. I was still figuring out what I wanted to do career-wise, thinking about moving all the way across the country, and had just made the hard decision to break up with my boyfriend. Since that relationship ended, I then started wondering who my future husband would be, so much was up in the air. My suggestion is this…Just take it one day at a time and surrender your plans and timing to God. His plans are for our good and His glory.

*What upcoming things in your life are bringing you anxiety today?
Surrender them to God.*

JOY IS COMING

"For I consider that the sufferings of this present time are not worth comparing with the glory that is to be revealed to us."
Romans 8:18

During the fall semester of my senior year in high school, I survived a tragic shooting where three students were killed, and others were injured. It marked the onset of a period of time that would challenge my mental capacity. A few months later, the 2020 COVID pandemic hit, canceling my birthday plans, my senior dance national championships, my senior prom, and my high school graduation. The pandemic continued that summer following all the cancellations. My Dad then experienced some numbness in his left shoulder while hiking and it turned out to be a blockage to one of the main arteries of his heart. He could have easily died had we not caught it in time and for God watching over him and the doctors during surgery. I went to college and because I was an athlete, I was allowed on campus for practices, but all my classes were online in my dorm. It was definitely a very odd beginning for an unconventional college experience. My sophomore year, COVID slowly started to fade, and I had my first serious relationship with my first boyfriend. Unfortunately, this didn't last long, and I then experienced my first breakup. A few months later, my dad was falsely accused of something he didn't do, weighing heavily on our family for over two years until his name was finally cleared. The summer before my junior year, I had my second boyfriend where this time I learned it hurts just as much to break up with someone as it does to be broken up with as I knew down deep that he wasn't the one for me. This led me to a third relationship that lasted on and off for over two years. It proved to be particularly toxic and mentally taxing. I also dealt with bullying in addition to a dose of "roommate drama." Then, within a very short period my Aunt Marcia, who was like a grandmother to me, passed unexpectedly while also discovering some questionable actions about the guy I was seeing.

Adding to that, I had made the difficult choice not to try out for dance during my senior year as I wanted to focus on acting. I followed through with my decision only to find out shortly afterwards that the whole industry would shut down for months due to the actors' and writers' strikes. I later dealt with significant acne and then a torn ACL. It seemed like ever since 2019, I just kept taking one hit after another and couldn't catch a break.

I experienced more things in just a few short years than most people would experience in their lifetime. At this point, it was difficult to have hope for the future. I had zero expectations and just assumed the worst. However, reminding myself that despite all those hardships, some have it much worse than me, and I'm still here today because of a good and faithful God. He got me through each and every single thing in His time and according to His plan. Even if there are more hard days ahead of me, I know He will help me through them. I find peace in knowing that ultimate joy isn't found in earthly comforts, material possessions, and smooth sailing throughout our lives. True joy will be my reward when after I have withstood the trials of this life, I hear the Savior saying, "Well done, good and faithful servant" as I enter heaven for all eternity. We have to keep remembering that God loves us more than we can ever comprehend. His word tells us in John 3:16, *"For God so loved the world, that He gave His only Son, that whoever believes in Him should not perish but have eternal life."*

Reflect on what hardships you have endured during your life and take time to pray and thank God for helping you through them. If you are currently in the middle of a hardship, seek comfort in knowing you aren't alone. God is with you, and if anything, our life here on earth is so short, that none of it will matter when we experience true joy in heaven.

28

BULLETPROOF

*"Fear not, for I am with you; be not dismayed, for I
am your God; I will strengthen you, I will help you, I
will uphold you with my righteous right hand."*
Isaiah 41:10

I'm sure you've heard the cliché that "God won't give you more than you can handle." Well, it's a nice phrase but that isn't exactly what you will see anywhere in the Bible. It does say in 1 Corinthians 10:13 that *"He will not let you be tempted beyond your ability, but with the temptation He will also provide the way of escape, that you may be able to endure."* The truth is, God will never give you more than He can handle, because He is the one who is with you guiding you through any trial in life. We're bound to see any number of challenges during our lives, and it is good to know that there is a God who is leading us through each of them.

There is also the popular cliche "God gives the hardest battles to His strongest soldiers" and this is very true. The closer your relationship is with God, the more the enemy is going to try to attack you and bring you down. The good news is, again, we know who wins in the end…God.

At this point, it feels like I've gone through so much that it seems like, "Bring it on! What's next?" Please understand that whatever you may be going through, God will be with you. He will give you strength. He will give you courage. And He will help you. You don't have to go through anything alone; He is always there for you. Two of my favorite verses in the Bible that speak to perseverance and protection are Philippians 4:13 that says, *"I can do all things through Him who gives me strength"* and Ephesians 6:11 which says, *"Put on the full armor of God."* With God by your side, you are bulletproof, and you can choose to be content, and you can get through anything.

Think about a time when God was there for you and helped you through something that seemed impossible. Thank Him for being by your side in every situation.

BE A LIGHT

"In the same way, let your light shine before others, so that they may see your good works and give glory to your Father who is in Heaven."
Matthew 5:16

One of my favorite YouTubers, Mary Sergi, a former cheerleader from the University of Alabama, has been a huge encouragement for me. If anyone could represent the embodiment of joy, surely that person would be Mary. Her smile and laughter are infectious. She cares about everyone around her. I love how open she is about her faith and her relationship with the Lord. She's simply a light that shines for Christ. With that said, it doesn't mean that Christ-followers don't have their dark days.

Mary has opened up on her Instagram regarding her past eating disorder, which she claims was one of the lowest points of her life. She said that "she was weak and unhealthy." She was working out a ton and hardly eating. Nothing mattered more to her than what she ate or looked like. She lived off the approval from others and achieving that "perfect" image in her head. She didn't like who she was, or how she looked, she felt alone, and "trapped." As someone who tends to have a bubbly personality, her friends could tell something was wrong with her as she wasn't herself. She was also away from family at the time for cheer, trying to do it all on her own, feeling so lost.

Like dancers and gymnasts, I know many cheerleaders who also struggle with their body image. Especially for Mary being a flyer, lifted in the air all day, worrying if she felt "too heavy" for her teammates could be mentally taxing. Mary's relationship with the Lord saved her from her eating disorder. Recovery didn't happen overnight, and it is still something she sometimes struggles with to this day. That reality played a big role in her making the decision not to cheer her last year at Bama. Sometimes you must do what is best for yourself and your mental health.

God has everything happen for a reason, and through all of this, Mary created a separate Instagram account @mare.cares, where she encourages and helps others who may be going through a similar situation by posting about her fitness journey and the food she eats. Mary states, "I now work out to feel stronger, I eat to nourish my body, and I live to do God's work." I love how Mary was able to bring light to a difficult time of her life, and to share with others how God helped her through a dark time. Keep shining Mary!

Think about today. How does Christ shine through you and your everyday actions?

30
THE BEST MEDICINE

"A joyful heart is good medicine, but a
crushed spirit dries up the bones."
Proverbs 17:22

The best "medicine" one could have is to have a happy heart, pray to God, and don't stress. Instead of stressing, keep your trust in Him. Something I have learned throughout my acne journey is how much stress actually impacts our health. It's mindboggling how everything in the body is linked together. Stress can throw off our hormones. There is a distinct correlation between our mind and gut and oftentimes poor gut health can be a contributor to acne, along with many other things.

One of the points I'm making throughout this book is, we need to be more kind to our bodies. There was a time when I was working out super intense all the time and being super restrictive with what I was eating, yet I was not seeing the results I wanted. I then learned more about women's bodies and our hormones and cortisol levels that play a crucial role in how we respond to stress. When I slowed down, doing lower impact workouts like Pilates, started using lighter weights with more reps, began speed walking on the treadmill, and nourishing my body more, I started to see the results I wanted because my cortisol and stress were lowered!

God created our bodies to be very smart, and sometimes our bodies will tell us something is wrong before our brain can even realize it. Towards the end of my two-year on-and-off relationship with my last boyfriend, that's when my face started to break out very badly. Stress! I should have recognized that as a major sign earlier. Your body shouldn't be in a fight or flight status if you're in the right relationship. We also have a God of peace, not confusion, and the right guy should make you feel calm and composed. My motto has always been, "When you meet the right guy, you'll glow."

Here's your reminder today to pray to God about whatever it is that's stressing you out. With stress weighing you down, it's easy to be crushed in spirit. Surrender and give it all to Him so you can live with a joyful heart.

31

FAITH IT TILL YOU MAKE IT

"Now faith is the assurance of things hoped for,
the conviction of things not seen."
Hebrews 11:1

This verse is very special to me as it is about my name, "Faith." It took my mom and dad nine years to have me; and through all that, came a lot of heartache, pain, waiting, and a large dose of faith… Faith that at the right time, God would make it happen. Similarly, we can't see God, but through faith, we know He's there with us. He's fighting our battles and interceding on our behalf regarding all our concerns. It's nice to know that He never takes time off. He's always working for us.

Sometimes I feel guilty for lacking faith in certain situations or for worrying and getting anxious. However, it is normal to feel that way; we are human. We are not wrong for feeling that way and it doesn't necessarily mean that we doubt God. In the Bible, it tells us all we need is faith the size of a mustard seed (Matthew 17:20). Do you know how small that is? It's not much! It may feel like you have lost all hope and have gone through so many trials, but don't lose faith. God has the perfect plan for you, and you need to trust His timing.

We've all heard the cliche "fake it till you make it;" but try replacing the word "fake" with "faith." Even when you don't feel like it, even when you can't see what the future holds, have faith; even if it's as small as a mustard seed.

Today, go get a grain of rice and put it on a spoon and just look at how small that really is. It is actually a little larger than a mustard seed. Let this be a reminder that if you have faith that small, that is all you need.

32

GOD IS CLOSER THAN YOU THINK

"The Lord is near to the brokenhearted and saves the crushed in spirit."
Psalm 34:18

Have you ever wished God would just sit down next to you and say, "this is what we're gonna do" and tell you exactly what the plan is amidst your current hardships? Sometimes it feels like despite all the reading of my Bible and praying, I still can't hear what God is telling me to do. I saw something the other day that said, "Whenever you feel like you can't hear the Lord, think, when someone is right next to you, you don't need to yell. Whatever you may be going through, know that God is right there. He sees all. He knows all.

Psalm 34:18 was the verse my mom found highlighted in her Bible one day when she was at her wits end trying to get pregnant . She had been crying so much and then she opened her Bible and found this verse. It immediately brought her a greater sense of peace. This verse also brought me comfort as I was on my acne journey. It seemed like I had tried everything and nothing was clearing my skin. The thing was each acne method took a certain amount of time and a level of consistency for it to "maybe" work. As it turned out in the end, it delivered miniscule results. I admit, I am very good at following a plan, as long as that plan is guaranteed to work. However, everybody is different; and with that comes trial and error. That is why I just wanted God to sit down with me and tell me what to do and then be patient, knowing that plan would work. God gave my mom a little girl at just the right time, and God cleared my skin at just the right time. He was right there with us through the waiting while we were experiencing that "crushed in spirit" feeling. Praise God for His grace and mercy as well as His many blessings.

Open your Bible today and highlight this verse, Psalm 34:18. Write it down on a notecard and memorize it. You never know when you may be having a rough day, and you may need to reference these words which, in turn, will bring you comfort.

33

A GOD OF MIRACLES

"For she said to herself, "If I only touch His garment, I will be made well." Jesus turned, and seeing her He said, "Take heart, daughter; your faith has made you well.""
Matthew 9:21-22

This verse comes from a woman in the Bible who had seen Jesus performing other miracles. She experienced incessant bleeding for a dozen years. She thought if she could just simply touch Jesus's clothes, that the bleeding would stop. She believed by touching Him she would be healed, and she was. However, it wasn't because she touched His clothes that she was healed, it was because of her faith in Him, knowing that He would heal her.

I can't even count the number of times I've prayed "Lord, please heal my skin." I had faith that He would heal me, it was more of a matter of when. I had been struggling with my skin condition for almost a year at this time. This struggle included countless prayers, countless tears, countless supplements, facials, skincare, and so on. I finally started this medication that was said to take about 10 to12 weeks to start kicking in, yet it took my skin just about 2 weeks to start seeing major progress. It felt like a miracle and too good to be true. For someone struggling with something for that long and to see such significant improvement that quickly brought me to happy tears and I was so thankful. Was it the medication? Yes, but it was also God. He is the ultimate healer, and He can work miracles.

Maybe you or someone you know is battling an illness or struggling with something right now. Pray to our Heavenly Father about it. Know that nothing is too big for Him. He may choose to heal or not to heal, however, He will give strength and hope to those who come to Him. And remember, God does perform miracles and can change things in a split second.

34

TRANSFORMED BODIES

"But our citizenship is in heaven, and from it we await a Savior, the Lord Jesus Christ, who will transform our lowly body to be like His glorious body, by the power that enables Him even to subject all things to Himself."
Philippians 3:20-21

If you have accepted Christ as your Lord and Savior and know that He died on the cross for your sins, and then rose from the dead three days later, you are saved. Salvation is yours. You have been redeemed and one day you will go home to Heaven to dwell in His presence for all eternity. After this life here on earth, you don't take anything with you. No one is backing up a U-Haul truck to fill it up with your stuff. You're not taking your money or your possessions. As a matter of fact, you're not even taking your old, worn-out body!

When we go to heaven, our bodies are made new. Heaven will be a place of no more insecurities, no more comparisons, no more jealousy, and no more illnesses. That is why, yes, you can get all the physical work done to yourself you want here on earth, but that quest for the perfect body results in leaving it behind later anyway. That's why I encourage you to instead work on your heart and soul, growing closer to Jesus, because that is all He cares about, and that is what will actually go with you to Heaven.

Seek comfort in knowing that whatever illness or insecurity you may be experiencing here in this imperfect world, will not last forever. We will be made new in Heaven, and things will be better than you could ever possibly imagine. So don't get so caught up in the things of this world because everything here is only temporary.

Instead of thinking about what you don't like about your body, change your mindset to your five senses. Thank God if you are able to see, hear, taste, smell, and touch.

35

IDOLATRY

*"You shall have no other gods before me. You shall not make for yourself
a carved image, or any likeness of anything that is in heaven above, or
that is in the earth beneath, or that is in the water under the earth."*
Exodus 20:3-4

The first of the Bible's ten commandments mentions, *"You shall have no other gods before me,"* says the Lord. Doing so is called idolatry. Many people when hearing this verse often think of materialistic items such as the golden calf in the Bible which the Israelites made their idol and worshipped. In the 21st century, idols are just as present although we don't have any golden statues of animals we worship. But we do find many who worship other worldly things, like money, cars, homes, certain possessions, your status, your job, your looks, and the list goes on.

Something I have been personally guilty of in the past is the amount of time I spent on dance. I didn't necessarily make it more important than God, but I spent so much time on it that it didn't leave much time for me to spend quality time with God. For many, it can be school, your job, or anything else that takes the place of time that could be spent with God.

Ever since retiring from dance as a collegiate athlete, I still workout about two hours a day. I have mentioned previously how I would exhibit a high level of OCD about things in life, including my workouts. I'm not saying that working out is bad because God has actually called us to take care of the bodies that He has given us. However, it is important to not make your body your top priority which could be taking away extra time that could be spent with God.

What "idols" are in your life and how can you keep God number one?

36

INTENTIONALLY MADE

"Before I formed you in the womb I knew you, and before you were born, I consecrated you; I appointed you a prophet to the nations."
Jeremiah 1:5

In Genesis, the first book of the Bible, we see that God created the heavens and the earth. On day one, He created light. On the second day, He created the sky. On the third day, He created the land, seas, plants, and trees. On the fourth day, He created the sun, moon, and stars. On the fifth day, He created creatures that live in the sea or fly. On day six, He created animals that live on earth and humans, made in His image. And on day seven, He rested. After all, that was a busy week!

Think about how God created all these things in six days, yet the Lord took nine months to create you in your mother's womb. The Lord took His time intentionally creating you just how you should be. Why change that? Whenever I feel insecure about something, I try to remind myself, God made me to be unique. No two people should be the same. Who am I to question how God made me to be?

Yes, there are things one can do to change their appearance. However, God loves you exactly as you are. He accepts your features no matter what imperfections you may have. In fact, he loves each and every single person on this earth and knows everyone by name. Even before He started to create you in your mother's womb, He knew you completely. Way before you were born, He knew exactly what your future would look like, down to every little detail. He knows your good deeds and He knows your sins. You were placed here for a reason, and ultimately, we are to help grow the Kingdom. You were intentionally made.

Think about the twelve months in one year. Think about the days in one month. Think about the days in one week. Think about the hours in one day. Think about the minutes in one hour. Think about the seconds in one minute. God knows and cares about every second of your life. Isn't that amazing to realize that He cares that much?

CLOTHE YOURSELF

"Put on then, as God's chosen ones, holy and beloved, compassionate
hearts, kindness, humility, meekness, and patience."
Colossians 3:12

As human beings, we are often materialistic and can get caught up in who has the newest, trendiest clothing, or the most expensive name brands. Many people often place importance on possessions rather than people. According to the scripture verse above, do you know what's even better to clothe yourself in? A heart that shows compassion and kindness towards others. Becoming one who is humble, meek, helpful, and considerate means so much more to our Creator than what designer brand bag you carry.

Do I like nice things? Yes, of course. Who doesn't? However, are you flaunting them around others, or do you display humility? Money can come and go, but do you know what remains through the years? Your heart. So, it stands to reason that we need to check the status of our hearts. A heart that is open to God's Word and produces a lot of fruit is a healthy heart. It's the main artery for the Holy Spirit to work through you.

Don't worry about fitting in with what everyone else is wearing. Instead, have a heart of gratitude for what God has provided for you. You know, most of the time, the people who have the most are actually the ones who are most unhappy. Money and clothes cannot buy happiness. In fact, the obsession often escalates to the point where a person is never satisfied.

At the end of the day, it doesn't matter what you wear on the outside. What truly matters are the qualities a person clothes themselves with on the inside. Guarding our hearts with carefulness is essential for our spiritual well being.

Look at all these words: compassion, kindness, humility, meekness, and patience. Pick one of those words and think about how you can "clothe yourself" in that word today. How can you best display that characteristic? Maybe go in your closet and look around. I am sure there are clothes you never wear that you can donate as an act of kindness.

MODESTY

"Women should adorn themselves in respectable
apparel, with modesty and self-control."
1 Timothy 2:9

Growing up, I was always the kid being "dress-coded" in elementary school. It wasn't that I was dressing inappropriately, I just had very long legs, so my skirts and dresses always appeared shorter. Granted, I did go to a private Christian school that had much stricter standards compared to those that are enforced on public school campuses. Additionally, being involved with dance almost from the moment I could walk, it seemed all I knew was "little" clothing. Dancers at the studio would always be wearing leotards and tights, "booty shorts" and a tank top, along with our dance costumes. I remember one time I had a dance competition in Las Vegas when I was very young (yes, Las Vegas). As my friends and I were walking past the casino to the ballroom where the competition was being held, my friends and I pointed out a cocktail waitress wearing an outfit that in our eyes also looked like a dance costume. I turned to my mom and said, "Mommy we look like her!" In my young and innocent eyes, I had no idea what was appropriate and what wasn't, I just viewed it as a dance costume. I am very blessed that my mom, along with many of the other dance moms at my studio, pushed for more conservative child dance costumes. They fought to have our midriffs covered and objected to costumes that could be seen as too risqué. As I got older and it was more appropriate for my age to wear a two piece as my attire on the dance floor, it was still very modest and classy.

I think for being a dancer my entire life, I've always just become used to wearing different outfits than those who were not brought up in a studio. For instance, I remember when I was little, going to the grocery store after practice and throwing on a ballet skirt over my leotard and tights. That didn't seem weird or unusual to me even though looking back, I must have appeared a little out of the norm to other shoppers. Now that I am no longer competing in dance, I have found myself in the acting and modeling industry where there can be a whole different challenge in terms of modesty. There have been job prospects offered to me where I was asked to play questionable roles that contradicted my spiritual values or wearing clothing that was far too revealing. I was even asked once if I would take a role as a "stripper." Of course, I declined those offers. I know it is very easy to get caught up in the Hollywood scene but selling one's soul to the devil for a chance for fame is not for me. I continue to look for roles that are morally fitting for my life as a Christ-follower. I know that sticking to my standards and remaining modest will bring more honor to God and that He in return will bless me in the future in other ways.

Consider what you wear daily out in public. Are those outfits bringing honor to God? Are they "trendy" or "trashy?" What should you change or add to your wardrobe to show yourself as more modest yet still fashionable?

39

IT'S OKAY TO ASK FOR HELP

"Bear one another's burdens, and so fulfill the law of Christ."
Galatians 6:2

When I was struggling with my hormonal acne, I was very stubborn and didn't want anybody's advice. If you have experienced acne, you know you have literally tried everything and have researched everywhere. You have thought about your acne every minute of every day and now someone wants to suggest something you've already tried that didn't work. It's annoying, yet you need to remember that person comes from love and is just trying to help.

It also doesn't help that I have always been a highly structured person where I like to know the plan and follow it. Not knowing the solution to my acne was driving me nuts! I've also always been very independent as an only child. It didn't help that I have an ego as a result and clearly didn't want to accept any help. In my early childhood days, when my mom or dad wanted to help me with a task, I would often say, "Myself" meaning stand back, I can do this.

However, life shouldn't be done alone, whether that be with your significant other, family, or friends. In addition to having God in your life, it is important to have a community around you. My mom always said that no matter where you live, if you can find a good church, the people there will be your community. We are called to be there for one another, during the good times and bad. But that also means there will be times when we need to accept help.

When I felt that I had exhausted all my options as I tried to heal my acne for almost an entire year holistically, I finally turned to others. I sought the advice of some family members and friends who were nurses and had told me about a medication to take that could potentially help. And wouldn't you know it, within just a few weeks my skin started clearing up! I realized that talking about my acne with close friends and family showed my vulnerability. It also brought up many personal stories that they had from when they had acne and hearing how they healed theirs. Acne is something most people experience. I still wouldn't say it's "normal" because it's an inflammatory response within the body saying something is off, but it is indeed very common. Sometimes it may be scary to share about what you're going through, but if you hold it within yourself, you miss out on the opportunity of receiving help from others. When Galatians 6:2 talks about "bearing one another's burdens," it means that we are called to help lift the weights off the backs of others.

If you are going through something difficult right now, consider reaching out to someone within your "community" to either talk or simply just have them be there for you. If your life is going great, that is wonderful! Think about the people in your community and check in with them and ask if there's anything you can pray for them or support them in any way.

40
REMEMBER TO THANK GOD

"Rejoice always, pray without ceasing, give thanks in all circumstances; for this is the will of God in Christ Jesus for you."
1 Thessalonians 5:16-17

When things in life are going great, praise God; when times are bad, praise God. We have an awesome God and He works all things for good (Romans 8:28). It is easy to be thankful when life goes well, but when times are tough, you have to really make an effort to look for those blessings in your life. And I can tell you this, you will always have more blessings than you can count.

I find myself crying and praying to God more than ever when I am going through a difficult time in my life. This is because I need Him. However, when things are going well, it can be easier to forget to spend as much time with God because you almost feel like you're good now. You may feel that you don't need Him as much. However, we will always need God whether it be in the good times or the bad.

When my skin suddenly started to clear within about two weeks, my self-confidence skyrocketed. I was back hanging out with friends, on movie sets, and I felt like I finally had my spark back. It almost seemed like I had already forgotten how many tears I shed and all that I had gone through in the past year. I think it's important to remember what we go through, not only for our own testimony, but to remain in a state of gratitude and thankfulness to God that we couldn't have gotten to where we are now without Him, and we will always need Him. Psalm 100:4 says, *"Enter His gates with thanksgiving, and His courts with praise! Give thanks to Him; bless His name!"*

Think about any difficult things God has helped you through in the past and take time to pray and thank Him. Look around you and remember to count your many blessings.

IT'LL BE FINE

"Cast all your anxieties on Him, because He cares for you."
1 Peter 5:7

My Aunt Marcia sadly passed away in February of 2023, which was an extremely hard time for me. I struggled mostly because I was so close to her, yet I was so far at the time because she lived in Kansas City, Missouri and I lived in California. I had to say my goodbyes to her through Facetime on the phone while she was lying in her hospital bed.

A few weeks later, we flew out to Kansas City for her funeral. It was a beautiful celebration of life because my Aunt Marcia was a very strong believer and would've wanted everyone at that funeral to join her in Heaven one day. The pastor said some nice things including a few scripture verses, but it was my dad who gave the eulogy and preached the gospel with fire and passion. We also understood that Aunt Marcia would not have wanted us to be sad about her passing. After all, we knew exactly where she had gone. She no longer walked by faith. She was now in the presence of Jesus and was reunited with all those loved ones who had gone home before her. Heaven was now her eternal dwelling place.

Everyone reflected on their favorite memories with her. Growing up, she was like a grandma to me as sadly both of my real grandmas had already passed. Aunt Marcia would bake with me, "cloud watch" with me, sneak me Cheetos and candy, and loved on me hard. She also cared so deeply for others. She would volunteer at the church where everyone knew her. She would also make pies or other goodies for the men at the fire and police stations, she would volunteer at the local food pantry, and so much more.

One of the things I think people loved most about her was she was always so happy. She had such an optimistic outlook on life no matter what the circumstance. Whenever someone was going through something difficult, she would encouragingly say, "Oh, it's fine" or "It'll be fine." How does she know that? Because she knew with her whole heart that God cares for each and every one of us. She saw God take care of her in tough times and knew that He would never leave or forsake her. She believed in Philippians 4:19 that says, *"My God will supply every need of yours according to His riches in glory in Christ Jesus."* So, give your worries to God, and He will bring you peace. Don't stress about it. No one adds a single hour to their lives by worrying (Matthew 6:27). That'll do nothing and it just takes away the joy that could instead be experienced that day. Surrender your cares and concerns to God and trust Him no matter what life throws at you.

I don't know what you are struggling with right now in your life, but I encourage you to practice my Aunt Marcia's "It'll be fine" attitude, trusting that God has already taken care of it. And if He hasn't yet, know that He will.

DON'T LOSE HOPE

"And He told them a parable to the effect that they
ought always to pray and not lose heart."
Luke 18:1

While watching the Paris 2024 Summer Olympics, my favorite sport to follow was our USA women's gymnastics team. Of course, who wasn't glued to their television sets when the GOAT, Simone Biles, took center stage? She won three gold medals! But remember back in the COVID delayed Tokyo Olympics in 2021 she suffered through some mental struggles and had to drop out of the competition. She obviously came back stronger than ever!

Another gymnast who caught my eye during the 2024 Olympics was Suni Lee and her story that she shared with the world. Lee was the reigning all-around Olympic champion and gold medalist from the Tokyo games but new developments since then changed her life. While training in 2023, just a year before the Paris Olympics, she woke up one morning incredibly swollen. It turns out she was diagnosed with an "incurable kidney disease." Her hands couldn't even fit into the grips, she was nauseous, couldn't train, and she had also gained considerable weight in the process. She considered retiring from gymnastics and even said in a *SELF Magazine* article, "Sometimes you don't even think you're capable of winning anymore."

However, she changed her mind-set and realized her story could inspire others. She refused to lose hope. She sought medical advice to help return her to health and started training again. Suni Lee ended up not just making the USA team and traveling to Paris, but she won another gold medal and two bronzes. Talk about a comeback! Before Suni won that gold medal in 2024, she held only a bronze. In an interview, she claimed that the bronze medal meant more to her than her previous gold medal because she didn't even think she'd make it to the 2024 Olympics after her kidney disease, let alone standing on the podium.

Suni's story is a testament that whatever you may be going through, don't lose hope. I can't speak to Suni Lee's faith beliefs, but as a Christ-follower myself, I know that when something seems hopeless, I pray. God can always turn things around. Something for me that seemed hopeless at the time was curing my hormonal acne. God healed me. I learned also that some things are just out of our control. As a result of her kidney disease, Suni gained almost 40 pounds, according to her article. Clearly that was out of her control.

Most would reason that it is easy to lose weight if you are eating in a caloric deficiency while combining a regimented fitness routine. Wrong. As a female especially, our bodies fluctuate throughout our cycles depending on where our hormones are at the moment. Sometimes this can lead to water retention where it appears that weight was gained. This is one of those things that is out of our control. It's how God made us as females. Maybe it's a health issue like Suni experienced. Remember you are beautiful in all stages of life, and although we might not always be in control of things fully, the Lord is. So, pray. Put your trust in Him, and don't lose hope.

What are you experiencing in your life right now that seems "hopeless"? Remember that nothing is too big for God. Pray to Him about what is bothering you and remember that He cares about every little thing that you care about or what takes up your thoughts.

43

JUST KEEP SWIMMING

"When you pass through the waters, I will be with you; and through the rivers, they shall not overwhelm you; when you walk through fire you shall not be burned, and the flame shall not consume you."
Isaiah 43:2

When I was thinking of a title for this devotion, I couldn't pass up the opportunity to use the iconic quote from Disney's *Finding Nemo,* "Just keep swimming." Sometimes, life just seems to overwhelm us. We are faced with various challenges and hardships. You just need to trust God and keep going, one foot in front of the other, step by step…just keep swimming!

Speaking of swimming, when I was watching the 2024 Paris Olympics, I saw some of the swimming events and I noticed a girl who had just won gold with a huge smile on her face. For me, as someone who was struggling with acne myself, I was more apt to notice hers. People are always going to notice things more when they are experiencing similar circumstances themselves. I think that perhaps had I not been so aware of my skin at the time, I may not have noticed hers. However, instead of feeling happy about winning gold, I felt bad for her that the entire world was seeing her acne on television. And obviously this isn't where hair, makeup, and editing are done, this was the Olympics!

I recognized this in me and quickly changed my perspective to seeing this girl as a role model for others. I loved that she was confident in who she was, not letting a little acne stop her from achieving something so monumental. When I had my acne concerns, I unfortunately felt the need to put my life on pause. I believed that I couldn't achieve anything when I looked inferior (granted there are still standards in the acting and modeling industry, but they also know how to apply makeup and edit). Don't let anything get in your way from achieving your goals. Keep on swimming and remembering that God is with you through it all.

Think big and ask yourself what goal you would like to achieve. Ask yourself what is stopping you or getting in your way? Pray to God that He would remove that obstruction and trust Him to help you achieve that dream.

44

TAKE CARE OF YOUR BODY

"Or do you not know that your body is a temple of the Holy Spirit within you, whom you have from God? You are not your own, for you were bought with a price. So, glorify God in your body."
1 Corinthians 6:19-20

I think more often than not, a person's motive for eating healthily and working out is to make our bodies become physically attractive. However, what if we changed that motive to being able to feel good and live a long and healthy life? Taking care of our bodies doesn't always have to be for vanity purposes. It can be because God has blessed us with only one body, and He expects us to take care of it during our lifetime. After all, He has a lot of plans for us and our bodies must hold up for the long haul.

This can mean getting seven to nine hours of recommended sleep every night. This could mean eating nutrient dense whole foods that give us proper fuel for our bodies. This could also mean working out and lifting weights (even if they're light) in addition to doing some form of cardiovascular fitness so that you still have enough strength and endurance to keep up with the grandkids one day.

God has called us here for a purpose which He Himself has designed for our lives. Among other things, we are to spread the gospel and love others. We cannot do any of that if our health doesn't allow it. We need to be good stewards of our bodies because God calls them temples. They are of great value to Him. After all, we were made in His image. Our bodies are the vessel in which we travel this life, loving and serving others, and being a walking testimony for Christ.

Reflect on how you are treating your body today? Are you fueling your body with foods that will set you up for success? Are you working out often and living an active lifestyle? Are you giving your body the rest it needs? What can you do differently this week to improve your body's health?

45

IT'S OKAY TO REST

"Come to me, all who labor and are heavy laden,
and I will give you rest."
Matthew 11:28

I don't know why, but it seems whenever I am traveling, I always come home sick. When you're on a trip, whether for work or for pleasure, it's easy to get out of your daily routine. Perhaps you are eating differently, and your workouts may not be quite the same as when you are home. Last year when I came home sick, my OCD was absolutely insane because I couldn't work out due to acquiring COVID. I am someone who likes routine and am generally very disciplined. As a result, I would get mad at myself for being off schedule or missing a workout. However, God always gives us exactly what we need to hear, and I kept seeing everywhere that it was okay to rest. Sometimes God determines that we need rest, and He physically shuts us down for a period of time. There is a time when to push yourself, and there is a time when you have no choice but to rest because your body won't get better without it. It is important to remember to give yourself grace just as God has given us.

It's also important to be thankful for times of rest. After my last relationship came to an end, along with graduating from college and battling through my acne issues, I felt completely exhausted, both physically and mentally. I was still busy with multiple jobs trying to build my career, and I was still working out and taking care of my body. But, for the first time in a long time, I felt peace. It was strange because it almost felt like boredom. I changed my perspective to thinking maybe the boredom I was experiencing was actually the rest I needed after being in a "fight or flight mode" for so long. My body had been so used to feeling "on edge" when a relationship ended, when I received my diploma, when things started to slow down, and when I finally achieved clear skin. I just felt tired. And guess what, that was okay! Give yourself more credit for all that you went through. Give yourself grace and know that this season isn't forever. So, take advantage of that "boredom" and the much-needed rest God is giving you right now.

Whether you are in a busy season of life or not, reflect on how you can give your body rest today. Is it going to bed a little earlier? Maybe it's just setting your timer for five minutes during your lunch break to take some deep breaths in silence with your eyes closed. Remember that it is okay to rest, your body needs it, and it is a command by God.

REJECTION

"I will never leave you nor forsake you."
Hebrews 13:5

We have all heard the cliche "rejection is redirection" or "rejection is God's protection," and both are so true. Whatever doesn't work out according to your plan, always know that God has something even better for you. This was a concept that was hard for me to grasp, being the person who is known for being a daily planner my entire life. Fully understanding it now has brought me so much peace. I go into everything giving it my all, and if it doesn't work out, I know that it wasn't God's will. Another cliche I often hear is "when it's God's will, there's no stopping it." This can apply to relationships, jobs, future events, and many other facets of your life.

This reminds me of the reason why my mom intentionally did not have me pursue acting, modeling, or pageants when I was younger. Little kids don't understand at that age what rejection is or why they weren't selected for a specific part. They may tend to think something was wrong with them, when really it was the unknown of what a judge, casting director, or modeling agent was actually looking for to cast the specific role. In return, this could severely and negatively alter the child's self-confidence which is still developing as they mature. As an adult, I am older and have already developed my self-worth, my confidence, and my identity in God. I know now that if I go on a casting call and it doesn't work out, it wasn't God's will. He also may have been protecting me from something.

This isn't to speak negatively against the acting, modeling, or pageant industry. I have been following influencer Lauren Norris for quite some time who never fails to make me smile watching her YouTube videos. I love how she uses her platform to uplift and encourage others by talking about her faith in God. She has competed in multiple pageants, as well as judging pageants. She speaks of how pageants are not always about beauty. She shares that it is also about truly getting to see the hearts of the girls competing and hearing their stories. Lauren is extremely vulnerable sharing at her pageants and on her YouTube videos about being diagnosed with endometriosis. Another woman who I follow that has been involved in pageants is Demi Tebow, Tim Tebow's wife. Demi was crowned Miss Universe in 2017 and was also Miss South Africa! She just recently wrote a book titled *A Crown That Lasts*. As amazing as it was winning those pageants, she realized that we are not our labels or titles. Our true worth and value come from God.

I don't know what you are going after at the moment. It could be that perfect job or a significant other but know that any rejection you face is truly God's protection, and He will redirect you. God will open doors, and close doors. He will give you more than what you lost or more than you could ever ask for. When it's God's will, there truly is no stopping it. Just be patient, and ultimately, out of all the rejections you may face in a lifetime, God promises that He will never reject you.

Think about something in the past that you thought you wanted but didn't get. Did God protect you from something? Did He give you better than you could ever imagine? Maybe you're still waiting for that item, or job, or person. I encourage you to keep praying. That day will come.

47

YOU DESERVE TO SHINE

"For am I now seeking the approval of man, or of God?"
Galatians 1:10

A lot of times, girls think they need to earn the approval of the guy they like. For me, I was actually very confident in myself and didn't really care what a guy thought of me. Some girls do their hair and makeup and pick out the perfect outfit to impress a guy, but I did all this stuff because it made me feel good. I did it for me.

I started to become less confident in myself during several relationships. It is natural for some men to have jealous tendencies and may not want you around other guys. I am embarrassed to say that I allowed others to influence some of my decisions. I was a collegiate dancer and one didn't like the fact that I was dancing in front of other guys. He often shared that he couldn't wait for me to graduate. He wasn't at my college with me and would make comments on my appearance saying, "I prefer you with no makeup." Other guys said that as well. I never really thought much about it and didn't really think anything of it during those times. It was perfectly fine with me because I knew that I was okay going with or without makeup as I grew up wearing it for dance competitions and I always wanted to take it off. I couldn't wait for my skin to breathe. However, personally, I like to feel put together when going out in public. I really didn't connect the dots until I saw that he, like a few others, started trying to control what I did or didn't do. A few wanted me to stop self-tanning, disregarding the fact that skin cancer runs in my family. From an early age I have had to be very careful getting a real tan in the sun. Others didn't like me having my eyebrows or nails done. And don't get me started on wardrobe choices. It just seemed like everything I did to make myself feel good, a guy had a reason that he wanted me to stop. FYI ladies, those are red flags! You do not need to have the permission, or the approval, from a man and I am so thankful that I stood up for myself and kept doing the things that I loved. I know that I do not need to do them, but I like to do them! They make me feel pretty and as a result, I feel even more confident in myself. I believe in the often-used mantra, "When you look good, you feel good!"

It seems like everyone is a content creator nowadays. There were many times when one guy had me be the person behind the camera. I remember hearing people walk by us commenting, "Why isn't she getting her picture taken too?" This made me laugh and feel better. However, the truth was that he didn't want to share the spotlight, and he didn't care that I also wanted to be in front of the camera. I was happy to help him, but I also wanted to shine, and I did not want someone to dim my light. I am thankful God protected me from several relationships, and they ended when they did. I also learned to never seek the approval of a man, or any other human being for that matter. Rather, I realized that the only one who truly matters is God and His approval.

Go treat yourself to some self-care today. Even if it sounds mindless or silly, don't worry about what others may think. Do something that makes you feel good.

48
BEING VULNERABLE

But He said to me, "My grace is sufficient for you, for my power is
made perfect in weakness." Therefore, I will boast all the more gladly
of my weaknesses, so that the power of Christ may rest upon me."
2 Corinthians 12:9

Something I learned during the time I was struggling with my skin condition was that insecurity can even ruin friendships and relationships if you allow it. At the time, I was so insecure about my acne that I often didn't feel like going out. I didn't tell my friends the reason why I often declined their kind invitations because I was too embarrassed. But now looking back, I should've just been honest with them because a lot of them easily could have thought I was just choosing to be distant or rudely disregarding them. Opening up about your vulnerability with something like this does take a lot of courage, but if you have true empathetic friends, they'll stick by your side regardless. I am so grateful my friends later understood. They even told me I looked happier. I started gaining my confidence back as my skin cleared up and I was finally exiting a very unhealthy relationship.

That relationship went on and off for two years. At one point, when I thought we were done for good, I started dating again. At this time, however, my hormonal acne started to pop up again and that quickly shut down my will to continue dating. One of the guys I met was really sweet who was so interested in me that he even binged all of my YouTube videos. As a result, he shared that he saw a future with me. Even so, I still turned him down because I wasn't in a time and a place for dating due to my own insecurities. Regardless, he would often tell me that I was beautiful. This proves yet again that I've never truly cared what a guy thinks of me as I have always been my harshest critic. I'm the one who cares how I look. It is important to know that you do not need a guy to make you feel confident. One's self-worth should never be found in a partner. It is important to be confident in yourself before starting a relationship. I knew I wasn't ready to start dating again at that point in my life and I knew that the only relationship that mattered to me was the one I had with Jesus.

As you often hear, "communication is key," I now realize that I should have communicated better with my friends and potential boyfriends who wanted relationships as to why I was being a distant friend or didn't want to continue dating. I am fairly certain that they all would have understood. In fact, being open and vulnerable can actually strengthen friendships and relationships. Even on social media where everyone appears to be perfect, it is important to not make it look like you have it all together. Apparently, a lot of people thought that of me when they had no idea how much I was struggling. After going through the trials of this past year I can now see that when you show others your weaknesses, and when you are authentic, it makes you more relatable and likeable. Even more so, God made us in His image but because of our sin nature, we have many flaws. When we are vulnerable and willing to open up about our hardships and challenges, we can share how He helped us through them. The truth that comes out of our struggle becomes part of our testimony which, in turn, can bring people to know Jesus.

If you are going through something alone right now, I encourage you to reach out to someone and talk about it. If life is going great, think about the people in your life and reach out to someone you know who is experiencing their own hardship. Invite them to meet up for lunch or coffee and remember to pray for them.

INFLUENCERS

"And He said to them, "Go into all the world and
proclaim the gospel to the whole creation.""
Mark 16:15

It seems that most everyone nowadays wants to have the title of an "influencer." This could mean sharing pictures from the restaurant where they ate, what they were wearing, or a current favorite product. It is one of the fastest growing jobs right now. Of course, most of the influencers with the greatest number of "followers" are often shown living in mansions in places like Beverly Hills and driving very expensive cars while wearing designer clothing. It is easy to see why everyone says, "I want to be like them!" Guilty! I, too, have been in the influencer world for over a year as I am writing this and have had the pleasure of working with multiple brands. I've been gifted free products, modeled clothes, given affiliate links to share with my followers, and have been paid for attending brand events. The thing is, it can quickly become an obsession. At first it is easy to be happy working with one brand until you see the next best brand and just want to keep working your way up until you're working with the top brands.

What if I told you that the top brand you could possibly be associated with as an influencer is actually for Jesus? We were called to this earth to share the gospel with others, not to share our OOTD (outfit of the day). Although being an influencer seems to be the way of the future, it is important to also hold ourselves accountable. The best way we can clothe ourselves in Christ is by living out how the Bible calls us to be and by being a representative of the Jesus brand in our daily lives.

How can you go out today and be an "influencer" for Jesus Christ sharing the gospel with others?

50

BEING PRETTY WON'T GET
YOU TO HEAVEN

"For God so loved the world, that He gave His only Son, that
whoever believes in Him should not perish but have eternal life."
John 3:16

We've all heard of the "pretty privilege" before; girls getting things just because they are physically attractive. Maybe it's the job, or the guy, or even letting the coffee be "on the house." Being pretty may come with its perks. Perhaps people might be nicer to you, or you may get invited to special exclusive events. But the one place your good looks won't get you is through the gates of Heaven.

The only way we can go to Heaven is by believing the gospel that Jesus Christ died on the cross for our sins He paid a price for our salvation that we couldn't pay on our own. His sacrifice, His grace, and His mercy were poured out when He was nailed to that cross. He died the death that was meant for us. But the real victory for Jesus and us was when He overcame the tomb and rose from death on the third day. Because He was alive, we can have the similar everlasting life. All we have to do is accept the free gift He offers us through His death and resurrection. Believe in Him and ask for forgiveness of your sins and repent. We are all born sinners. Nobody is perfect. It's about making a conscious effort every single day to live your life according to God's word.

You will either go to Heaven or you will spend eternity in hell when you die or when Jesus comes back. We don't know when He will return, so we need to be ready! Accept Christ into your life today, not tomorrow, and start living your life in a way that honors Him. Don't let anything come before God. Surrender your life to Him. Whatever is sitting on the throne of your soul needs to go. Jesus needs to be most important.

What is sitting on the throne of your soul that needs to go? Your wardrobe? Your body? Your job title? Name brands? Whatever it is, pray to God to help you release it and to put Him at the forefront of your mind and heart.

51
ONLY ONE GOD

*"For although there may be so-called gods in heaven or on earth – as indeed
there are many "gods" and many "lords" – yet for us there is one God, the
Father, from whom are all things and for whom we exist, and one Lord,
Jesus Christ, through whom are all things and through whom we exist."*
1 Corinthians 8:5-6

Something I love about being a girl is doing my makeup each day. It's like a
form of therapy as I sit at my vanity having "me time," while either listening
to a podcast or music as I am getting ready. The only negative thing about
makeup is if you have gone to Sephora, Ulta, or wherever else you may get
your makeup, you are aware that it is not cheap! That being said, everyone
loves a good "dupe." For those that don't know, the word "dupe" comes from
the word duplicate, for instance a makeup item that is very similar to another
one you like, but slightly different and perhaps a little less expensive.

As much as we might like a good "dupe" from time to time, let's be very
clear, there is no "dupe" for God the Father. In 1 Corinthians 8:5-6, we see
it says, "one God" and "one Lord," not many. Yes, there are other "gods" that
people may put on their pedestals and choose to worship here on this earth
like money, power, prestige, possessions, and many others. But ultimately
there's only one true God. He is the Father, Son, and the Holy Spirit - three in
one. (Ephesians 4:4-6). He is holy and perfect. He is righteous and pure. He
is the author of love. He is also a just judge who will one day judge the world.

*Next time you get a "dupe" of something, let that be a reminder that there
is no "dupe" for our God. He is the "King of Kings" and "Lord of Lords."
(Revelation 19:16)*

GIVE IT TO GOD

"Therefore, since we are surrounded by so great a cloud of witnesses,
let us also lay aside every weight, and sin which clings so closely,
and let us run with endurance the race that is set before us."
Hebrews 12:1

Back when my parents were in their twenties, my mom would say that if they wanted to learn something about a specific topic, they'd have to browse through books by either going to the library or looking through their encyclopedias. It is amazing how we have information right at our fingertips today. Within seconds, we can find things just by typing a few key words into our phones. This, however, has its pros and cons.

I am someone who is very guilty of looking things up on WebMD. The second I have a symptom of something, I am looking it up! And guess what pops up? The worst-case scenario that turns out far from what I had. It just made me overreact and began worrying for nothing.

Anxiety can really weigh us down. That's why I chose to use the scripture verse above from Hebrews 12. Notice how it tells us to "lay aside every weight" so we can "run the race set before us." We are commanded to let go of the struggles we face. Lay them aside and allow God to do what He does best... orchestrate our lives with excellence. Whether the struggles you are facing are financial, dealing with relationships, job related, or some other kind of fear, you must let God do what only He can do. When those weights are cast aside from burdening us down, we are then able to run the race that God intends for us. We can pursue the purpose for which our Savior has for us.

When I was on my hormonal acne journey, I was constantly worried and always researching for answers. That, in and of itself, was a terrible weight on my shoulders. One positive thing that did come from this over excessive thirst for knowledge caused me to love learning about health. However, it's important to note where you are obtaining your information. I would fall down rabbit holes looking at Reddit or TikTok bringing in people's opinions and/or experiences on certain medications for their acne and the positive and negatives with each. However, everybody is different and, therefore, some will have different experiences than others. Again, one shouldn't compare oneself to others.

Instead of overwhelming yourself looking things up on your phone, ask yourself, have you prayed about it? Have you surrendered the situation and given it to God? It is important to remember that God isn't one of those genies in a bottle. However, I can tell you that there's nothing too big or too small that God doesn't care about when it comes to you. You are one of His precious children.

After turning off your alarm each morning, I'm sure the first thing a lot of people do next is to grab the phone and start scrolling. Do you really want to start your day off by comparing yourself to others? I encourage you to set up your day for success by ignoring your phone for at least half an hour when waking up. Do your morning routine, go outside, pray to God. Thank Him for another day, read your Bible, make some coffee. Whatever it is, do that instead of reaching for the phone.

53

PURPOSE BEHIND THE PAIN

"Jesus answered him, 'What I am doing you do not
understand now, but afterward you will understand.'"
John 13:7

When I was young, I remember going on a field trip with my school to the organization "Joni and Friends" founded by Joni Eareckson Tada.

On July 30th, 1967, when she was 17 years old, Joni dove into the water at Chesapeake Bay, misjudging how shallow the water was. She fractured her spinal column and was paralyzed from the shoulders down. She had two years of rehab where she claims she experienced depression, anger, religious doubts, and even had suicidal thoughts.

When bad things happen to us, it's easy to question, "Why God?" Sometimes, you don't see it yet, but He will use your pain for a purpose. Joni could've died that day, but she lived. During occupational therapy, she learned to paint by only using her teeth to hold and guide the paintbrush! Talk about making the most of what you are given by using what you have that still works. When she's not using voice recognition technology, she can also write with her teeth.

As I am older now, I can look back at her story and have a completely different viewpoint. I can see things from a different perspective, especially when I am feeling insecure about my body. God blessed me with two arms, two legs, and a healthy body that can move and function. Not all people can say the same.

Because of Joni's story, she started "Joni and Friends" which is a Christian organization advocating for others with disabilities. They are known to help provide wheelchairs for the needy around the world. She has also written over 40 books, recorded multiple music albums, starred in a movie about her life, hosts her own radio show, and is an amazing artist (doing so by using just her teeth). She does have minimal use of her hands and still experiences chronic pain.

We take so much for granted while we journey down this pathway of life. We always assume that we will have things like healthy eyes to see, ears that can hear, voices that can speak, and arms and legs that can move. For many who have specific disabilities, they easily could focus on what they don't have and dive deep into the depths of depression. We can learn a lot from those like Joni Eareckson Tada who choose to go a different direction. She has taken what she has, even after losing so much, and gives thanks to God for opportunities to tell the world about how awesome He is and how blessed she is. She would be the first to tell you that sometimes in life, there's purpose behind the pain.

I don't know what you are going through right now but know that God does everything with a purpose whether you see it yet or not. In the meantime, be like Joni and don't let your situation hold you back. She was able to accomplish and do so much with what she was given, and you can as well. God can and will use you too. If you're in a season of life right now where you aren't experiencing any hardships, take a moment to be extra grateful for what you have been blessed with as others haven't been as fortunate.

54

SPRINKLE LIFE WITH CONFETTI

"Rejoice in the Lord always; again, I will say, rejoice."
Philippians 4:4

One Sunday at Way Church, Pastor Noah told a story about he and his wife, Maddy driving on a road, when suddenly the wife (who was driving) pulled over off to the side. He started questioning what happened. "Did we hit something? Did a tire blow?" Nope. She got out of the car simply because she saw some pretty flowers that she wanted to pick. That is what she called, "sprinkling life with confetti."

Pastor Noah went on to explain how his wife's phrase "sprinkling life with confetti" means taking time out of your day to find gratitude or joy in something that is small and often overlooked. She was committed to watching for those small moments each day. So much so that she has a reminder set on her phone every day asking if she's "sprinkled her confetti" yet that day. I love this so much! There are so many things in life that we take for granted, and it's nice to take a step back and truly appreciate those things and thank God.

When was the last time you went for a walk and felt the sun on your face and heard the birds singing? That's confetti. How about the smell of your mom's freshly baked pumpkin bread filling the house as you decorate for Christmas? That's confetti. It's important to realize that "confetti moments" are all around us. We must take the time to open our eyes and see them. We tend to get too caught up in the busyness of life to fully enjoy the specialness of living.

The quickest way to turn a bad day or situation around is to count your blessings. Even on the hardest, most difficult days, there will always be something to be thankful for as our blessings far outnumber our trials. This may be a reminder as to why the Lord tells us to rejoice always!

Think today, how can you "sprinkle confetti?" If you want, go ahead and set a reminder on your phone as well to "sprinkle confetti" every day.

55

THE WAY IS JESUS

"But God shows His love for us in that while we
were still sinners, Christ died for us."
Romans 5:8

I don't know when you may be reading this devotion, but my favorite time of the year is Christmas. Yes, of course, there are presents, Christmas lights, decorations, hot cocoa, cookies in the oven, the fireplace lit on that cold day, being around family, and so much more. However, it is ultimately the time when we received the best gift of all, Jesus Christ, who was born a humble birth in a manger. He was brought into this world for one purpose…to later die a death on a cross to save us all from eternal separation from God. Those little, tiny hands that were born in Bethlehem, would be pierced by large nails at the cross. This all sounds horrible but it only magnifies the love that God has for us, His children. Without the manger, there is no substitute for our sin. Without the cross, there is no payment for our sin. And without the resurrection, there is no victory over our sin. That's the message of Christmas…Christ with us. Jesus is the way!

One of my favorite Christmas movies to watch is The Grinch (2000) with Jim Carrey playing the role of the Grinch. I know, it sounds silly. I guess in a way, I always related to Cindy Lou Who who was always trying to see the good in all people. She cared for the Grinch despite what he looked like or what other people's opinion was of him. She saw the good in him. She saw what he could be, and by the end of the movie, his heart grew three sizes that day. Just as Cindy Lou Who saw the Grinch and his potential, that's how God sees us. God's love for us isn't determined by our appearance, our status, or our wealth. He isn't impressed by those worldly things. He wants our heart, and he wants us to repent of our sins. He wants us to do an about-face, to turn from our evil ways, and start loving others as ourselves, as mentioned in Matthew 22:39 and again in Mark 12:31.

Jim Carrey is an A-list actor, featured in many films, and has made quite a career for himself. However, what makes him so commendable is his recent reality statement, "I think everyone should get rich and famous and do everything they ever dreamed of so they can see that it's not the answer." Jim Carrey has given his life to Jesus which is amazing as it isn't as common to find Christ-followers in Hollywood. When I see someone use their platform to spread the word of God, it makes me so happy. Getting "rich and famous" is not the way for a better life, there will always be holes to fill. The only way is Jesus Christ. Only He can satisfy your soul.

What is consuming your life and your thoughts right now? Is it your appearance? Your finances? Your career? Your status? Whatever it is, surrender it to God because none of those things will matter in the long run. Jesus will fill that void, and He is the only way to eternal life.

56
UNCONDITIONAL LOVE

"I have loved you with an everlasting love; therefore
I have continued my faithfulness to you."
Jeremiah 31:3

I saw something the other day on social media that said, "I love her because her stomach is flat," "I invited her because she has no cellulite," "I love her because she's a size 6," "We're friends because she denies food when she's hungry," "I talk to her because her thighs don't touch," "I think she's so cool for not eating all day," "We're best friends because she fits into those small jeans," … "said no one ever." I love this because it is so true, yet these are statements many of us, especially girls, think in our heads daily about ourselves.

We are all our own harshest critics, and I can tell you for sure, nobody is thinking about you but yourself. To be perfectly honest, most people are often so caught up in worrying about themselves and what others may be thinking about them that they aren't even thinking about your insecurities and misconceptions. And even if they are thinking about those things about you, then they aren't the right friend or significant other and you should probably re-evaluate who you are surrounding yourself with. My dad always told me, "Show me your friends, and I'll show you your future." It is true, we tend to become like those whom we surround ourselves with.

The good news is, even if you have nobody, you will always have somebody… a somebody that cares about you for who you are… a somebody who will never leave you… a somebody we call our Heavenly Father, our God, and our Comforter. There is nothing you could ever do that will make God stop loving you. He doesn't care about your appearance or any of your insecurities for that matter. His love for you is unconditional and everlasting.

Take a moment today to evaluate who you are surrounding yourself with. Are they uplifting or tearing you down? Take time to also thank God for His never-ending love for you.

PRAY HARD

"Whatever you ask for in prayer, believe that you
have received it, and it will be yours."
Mark 11:24

When reading this verse, it is important to keep in mind that God is not one of those genies in a bottle; He doesn't simply give you everything you ask for. In fact, sometimes He has something much different and even greater for you than what you desire. Most people have heard of the saying, "God will give you back better than what you lost." That can be true but sometimes He may give you something more than what you have been asking for in the waiting. God's timeline is not our timeline and oftentimes we are called to be patient. The circumstances might not change immediately or ever, but you can change. One great way to help with the waiting is getting into God's Word each day. It's always a good idea to find a consistent time during the day where you can dive deeply into the scriptures and catch glimpses of what God wants you to hear. You'll often gain a whole new perspective on the things that are challenging you at the time. It also helps us remember who is in control. Giving everything to the Lord and focusing only on controlling what we can control is helpful. Keep praying to Him and not just say the usual words, but truly talk to God. Share your heart. Give Him praise and allow Him to work in your life. Believe that God will bless you with what you are praying for and will always have a better plan for us than we could ever imagine.

Have you ever had a kid ask you for something and you kind of choose to have selective hearing until they ask again, and again, and again, until you make provisions to give them what they want? Now I'm not advocating for the "squeaky wheel gets the grease" scenario but I do want you to know that we need to be consistent and intentional with our prayers to the Heavenly Father. Don't just pray once over that which you are requesting, but instead pray continuously. There is real power in prayer.

When I was struggling with my acne concerns, I prayed with heavy tears to God every day for more days than I can count. Finally, I saw the light at the end of the tunnel and my skin began to clear. It took time and persistent prayer. I'd say the whole journey took a little over a year, and now I look back, even though it was extremely hard, I'm grateful that God didn't just give me what I wanted right away because I wouldn't have been as appreciative. God's timing is always perfect. In the waiting, I learned so much and continued to grow in my faith. I became more empathetic toward others and am in a place now where I hope to help others who may be going through similar hardships and challenges. As a matter of fact, this devotional most likely would not have been written had God answered my prayers right away.

Remember too that just because you got what you wanted doesn't mean that you should stop praying to God. Instead, remember to thank Him! You need Jesus when life is hard, and you also need Jesus when life is good. Trust Jesus during the storm, but also be alert when things are going well because the devil wants to tear you down. Things can change in an instant. You never know what might be around the next corner. Whatever stage of life you are in right now, you need Jesus. Every. Single. Day. Pray. Hard.

What is something you have been praying for lately? Ask yourself, have you been praying consistently for that thing? Start today being intentional of reminding God what is on your heart.

58

SELFLESS

"Let no one seek his own good, but the good of his neighbor."
1 Corinthians 10:24

As a very planned out person, I always thought of myself getting married around the age of 23 and having kids by 25 years of age. Granted, I'm only 22 right now as I am writing this so I suppose that the timeline could still play out, but the likelihood would be small. I just went through a breakup, and I finally found the right medication to make my skin clear. The following is going to seem extremely vain, but my goal in this devotional has been to be as transparent as I can possibly be. I've always wanted kids, but I have always been concerned about how much my body would change in the process. Looking back at how much I went through mentally and physically with my hormonal acne issues, I don't want to stop this medication anytime soon. If I wanted to become pregnant, I would have to stop using it. As a result, my skin would likely start breaking out to some degree and gaining a ton of weight usually goes hand in hand with pregnancy. Full disclosure... that scares me.

I've talked to my mom about these things, and she reminds me that all of that would be temporary. I could go back on my medication after having a baby and my clear skin would return. Also, pregnancy weight can be lost rather quickly if one breast feeds and is intentional about trying to return to their pre-baby body. My mom also reminded me that it took her nine years to get pregnant with me and she had to get hormone injections daily, her whole body was swollen with water retention. She gained 70 pounds! All while working out every day, eating super healthy with lots of broccoli, no caffeine, etc. Let's just say, her hospital pics weren't like the Instagram hospital pics we see today of the moms with their hair and makeup done and their newborn baby in their arms. But she says all the time, I was absolutely worth it. She always tells me that I was the result of many prayers.

Despite all that my mom went through to have me, she says she wouldn't have changed a thing. I came at the right time, and I was worth the wait. Looking at all she had to endure, the waiting, the crying, the injections, the weight gain, all I can see is selflessness in her. And she's right, all that was temporary and she ended up being such a beautiful momma to her sweet baby girl. Even today, she is still the epitome of putting others before herself, just as God has called us, and I pray I can be half the mom she is one day.

How can you practice selflessness today? Start small as it can be as simple as letting someone go in front of you in line at the grocery store which can lead to bigger acts each day.

HUMILITY

"Humble yourselves before the Lord, and He will exalt you."
James 4:10

There have been many times where I have looked back on pictures of me in the past during my awkward years. I would often ask my mom, "Why on earth did you let me wear that?" She would respond, "You felt confident at the time." I'm sure even now when I'm feeling confident in how I look, I'll look back in the future and be critiquing my outfit or my look in some way. However, you know what never goes out of style? Being humble.

Showing humility is such an attractive quality, but being boastful can instantly ruin that image. Scripture tells us in Proverbs 16:18 that "Pride goes before the fall." I'm sure we're all guilty of such arrogance but God warns of what can happen when we have a self-centered heart. I really saw it firsthand with one of my past relationships. I would find myself getting secondhand embarrassment from him. He would often boast about his past accomplishments when people didn't even ask. Or he would share how amazing he was because he did this or that. That is one good thing about breakups; you can reflect on what you do want and don't want in your future partner.

When I visited Nashville, Tennessee I met some very sweet guys who were extremely humble. It was noticeable to see how the Lord had blessed them with so much! One had a family YouTube channel with over 12 million subscribers and 5 million on Instagram, far more than anyone I ever knew. However, the numbers weren't what impressed me, it was how they used their platforms to spread God's word. There's a huge difference between showing people what the world wants to see, "Hey look what I'm doing!" vs "Look what God is doing!" God calls us to promote Him not ourselves. Very little of what we accomplish can be done without God, and when we live in humility, God may use us even more.

I also met a young pastor named Noah Herrin at Way Church in Nashville who started his own church. He founded the church, and it grew tremendously from 6 people attending to filling three Sunday services after only 12 months of existence! He travels multiple times a year to speak at other churches as well. He has around 100k followers on Instagram which may not be as much as some others, but the Bible says we are hoping to hear the words, "Well done, good and faithful servant," (Matthew 25:23), not "Well done, good and famous servant." The Lord has blessed him with an amazing family of his own, and the opportunity to impact many people's lives in coming to know Christ. I am certain he feels that his calling is certainly not only rewarding, but a spiritual blessing.

It also says in the Bible that "one who is faithful in very little is also faithful in much" (Luke 16:10). The Lord will bless those who remain humble and want to show how God has used them through their circumstances. Clothe yourself in humility as pride is never attractive.

Ask yourself, if your friends or family could describe you, would they think you are a humble person, or constantly bragging about yourself? If your answer is the latter, how can you modify your actions?

COMPETITION

"A tranquil heart gives life to the flesh, but envy makes the bones rot."
Proverbs 14:30

I must admit that my senior year of college was certainly way out of the norm. I experienced such an extremely high level of insecurity that it made me very anxious. I believe it is generally more normal for most junior high or high schoolers to experience these kinds of acne issues but mine took place later in life. It took me awhile to understand all this because I was always busy dancing from a very young age. My worth back then was not found in how I looked, but how well I could dance compared to those around me.

Once I retired from dance, I no longer had that sense of competition. Instead, my new competition focused on others in the modeling or acting industry. Yes, perhaps talent was involved, but it was mostly based on what kind of look was needed. This quickly evolved into a new kind of competition, one that is based on who could have the clearest skin, the right look, the fittest body, the thinnest figure, the best hair or eyes, etc.

I have some friends who have competed in body building competitions, something I would never care to do. However, I do remember hearing their stories of how disciplined they had to be with their training and diets. They were so strict that they stuck to only eating brown rice, chicken, and broccoli (which is basically my daily meal anyways), and depriving themselves from sweets (which I was also doing because I feared sugar breaking out my skin). In a sense, I guess I could relate to them. On the day of their competition, afterwards, they would finally get to eat all the unhealthy food they wanted, literally crying tears of joy. It's no surprise that many talk about how this lifestyle can really mess with one's mental health. It is sad to think that maybe the medal was won, but at what price? It may have come with the price of extreme OCD. One's social life may have been sacrificed by spending multiple hours in the gym, avoiding certain foods, and, as a result, battling self-sabotaging demons affecting one's mental health.

Life isn't supposed to be a competition. Life is already hard enough. It is important to be supportive of one another. I was never the best dancer, but I did have the best work ethic. To this day, I remember when I was young, and my best friend won the dance competition we were in. Without even being told by my parents, I went up to her and gave her the biggest congratulatory hug. I think my parents honestly were more emotional than me for not winning, but their hearts quickly changed to being incredibly proud as they saw their little girl do this heartfelt act of kindness. I still have this moment captured in a framed picture and it's one of my favorites.

All of this is not to say healthy competition is bad, especially when it comes to sports. Afterall, I am very honored to walk away from my college team saying I am a three-time Division 1 Collegiate National Champion in dance. However, I didn't know that was going to happen, I just always gave it my all, using the gifts God had blessed me with, and He knew the outcome. As stated in previous devotions, "comparison is the thief of all joy." Don't be in competition with one another, instead, be there for one another, and remember to always give your best.

Are you mentally competing with anyone right now? If so, I encourage you to pray to God to help you drop it and learn to be content with who and where you are right now, being the best "you" that you can be.

61
REFLECT THE WORD

"Love is patient and kind; love does not envy or boast; it is not arrogant or rude. It does not insist on its own way; it is not irritable or resentful; it does not rejoice at wrongdoing but rejoices with the truth. Love bears all things, believes all things, hopes all things, endures all things."
1 Corinthians 13:4-8

Without looking in a mirror, your phone, or a reflection of any kind, try to look at your face. You can't. It is impossible to see yourself without those aids. However, the Word of God allows us to see our faces spiritually. The more you read the Bible and spend time in the Word, the more you'll see how desperately you need Jesus Christ. Your sins will be illuminated, and it will be apparent how much you need the Lord in your life.

We should read the Word and then aim to reflect it. A good personal check of this is to look at today's verse and replace your name with each time it says the word "love" or "it." For instance, I will insert my name, "Faith is patient and kind; Faith does not envy or boast; Faith is not arrogant or rude. Faith does not insist on her own way; Faith is not irritable or resentful; Faith does not rejoice at wrongdoing but rejoices with the truth. Faith bears all things, believes all things, hopes all things, endures all things." Now think to yourself, are these statements true? I'll call it right now that nobody is saying they reflect all those statements as we were born sinners and are imperfect human beings and there is always something we could work on to improve.

Instead of spending so much time in the mirror looking at your reflection and improving your physical appearance, make sure you are spending just as much time reading your Bible and practicing the more meaningful spiritual reflection of how Christ calls us to live our lives. In closing, I like what

1 Peter 1: 15-16 tells us regarding our living as Christ. It says, "*but as he who called you is holy, you also be holy in all your conduct, since it is written, 'You shall be holy, for I am holy.'*"

Which statements out of today's 1 Corinthians 13 verse could you work on to improve?

62

DON'T TAKE MORE THAN NEEDED

*"Be not among drunkards or among gluttonous eaters
of meat, for the drunkard and the glutton will come to
poverty, and slumber will clothe them with rags."*
Proverbs 23:20-21

Have you ever set a New Years goal to finally lose that weight or clean up your diet? What I have observed is that many people go in with an all or nothing mindset. Perhaps they completely cut out carbs or sugar. In doing so, come February, their goal is out the window because they were too restrictive and caved when they had a craving for the foods they had missed. Oftentimes one might over-indulge and binge due to this all or nothing mindset.

I was very restrictive during my hormonal acne journey because I had heard so many things which could cause my skin to break out. Luckily, being a certified wellness coach and knowing about balanced 80/20 eating (80% whole foods, 20% "fun" foods) while also still being very disciplined, I didn't overeat all the restricted foods I had missed. Instead, I slowly incorporated them back into my diet, having things here and there, intuitively eating, yet not overdoing it.

What some people may not even realize is that gluttony is a sin. In the Bible, God promised to provide the Israelites with bread each day, however, if they took too much, it would go bad. They should only take as much as they needed that day while trusting that God would provide for the days to come. Jesus commands us to take care of our bodies. That means both making sure we fuel our bodies with enough food, but also not overeating and taking more than your body needs.

What do your eating habits look like? Are you taking care of the body God has blessed you with?

63

YOUR CIRCUMSTANCES DON'T DEFINE YOU

"But now thus says the Lord, he who created you oh Jacob, he who formed you oh Israel, fear not, for I have redeemed you. I have called you by name, you are mine. When you pass through the waters I will be with you, and through the rivers they shall not overwhelm you. When you walk through fire you shall not be burned, and the flames shall not consume you. For I am the Lord your God, the holy one of Israel, your savior."
Isaiah 43:1-3

D on't identify more with your struggles than you do with your name. Just like the woman in the Bible who was known for bleeding, when I was struggling with my hormonal acne, I was very guilty of letting that define me and have that as my identity.

Did you know that everyone is going through something in their life? You can see some problems but some you may not. In the woman's case in Mark 5:25-34, people knew she was bleeding. Many believed that this would also happen to them if they came in contact with her. As a result, everywhere she went people would either back away from her or even yell at her to stay away. This poor woman was truly alone given her circumstances. However, she had enough faith to know that Jesus could heal her if she touched his garments. When he asked who had touched him the woman came forward and he referred to her as daughter. He said, "Daughter, your faith has made you well; go in peace, and be healed of your disease." We may go through challenges in life but when we know Jesus as our Savior, we aren't going through these battles alone.

We don't know this woman's name in the Bible, and the chances are, not many people back then knew her name either, but they knew she was the one who was bleeding. I could relate to her situation everywhere I went. I thought of myself as the girl who had terrible acne instead of seeing my true worth. Thoughts have power. Don't believe the lies the devil wants you to believe, rather remember whom you belong to. It is already hard enough to live in this society where the world wants to take your life and your thoughts captive. It is important to intentionally try to live like Jesus getting to know Him through scripture and daily prayer. Those thoughts add up and don't we all want to lead a life living intentionally to glorify God?

Be mindful of how you are speaking to yourself today. Are you picking yourself apart and believing the lies the devil wants you to believe? Or are you speaking positive affirmations to yourself based on what God shares in His word? Remember YOU are God's chosen daughter.

64

DON'T LEAN ON YOUR OWN UNDERSTANDING

*"Trust in the Lord with all your heart, and do
not lean on your own understanding."*
Proverbs 3:5

When I was little, I remember a special assembly at my private Christian elementary school. The guest speaker was Nick Vujicic. For those reading this who don't know Nick's story, he was born December 4th, 1982, with tetra-amelia syndrome, meaning he was born with the absence of all four limbs. However, God gave him the gift of a small foot on his left hip which he refers to as his "chicken foot" which helps him balance, kick, type, write, and even pick things up! I remember watching him in awe. It was so cool to see a simple task achieved, like picking up a phone, with the little foot that he had. Yet, God gave him enough.

Nick has become a phenomenal public speaker. He travels the world, impacting many people's lives by sharing his story. When Nick was eight years old, he was extremely depressed, largely because he felt like a failure and was being bullied by other kids at school. Two years later when he was ten, he tried to take his own life by drowning himself as he felt like he was simply a burden to his family. I want everyone reading this to know that NOTHING is too big to end your own life, and nothing is too big for our great and awesome God. Nick would soon see how much God loves him and what He had planned for his life.

If only ten-year-old Nick could have looked at the future and seen all the lives he would one day impact. Sometimes, we can't see why God is having us endure certain things, but as God's Word says, *"lean not on your own understanding,"* because everything He does is for good. Nick has spoken at live events, in prison ministries, to many student populations, at prayer ministries, and at "the Big Jesus Tent." He has spoken in over 57 countries and at well over 3,000 events. He speaks primarily about overcoming obstacles. He reminds everyone that with God's help you can overcome anything. Additionally, he shares about being confident, raising awareness about bullying, inspiring positive change, and to having determination and persistence all with God's help. Nick is now married, and they have been blessed with two healthy boys and two healthy girls. He has also written a number of books, received many awards, and has even appeared in movies. Having been born in Australia, young Nick was not allowed to attend any mainstream schools due to his disability as dictated by their state laws. However, the law was changed, and Nick can now say he was the first physically disabled student to attend a mainstream school in Australia!

Nick truly made a mark on so many people, all from a place where he initially saw no hope for the future. God can turn any situation around and use it for good. It may not be the way we might have envisioned, but God always has a better idea. You may not understand it all now, but all you need to do is lean on God and trust Him.

Take a moment to sit down and pray to God, thanking Him for all He has blessed you with, even if you may feel like you have nothing. There is always something to be thankful for. Then ask God to help you see hope for a future, despite whatever you may be going through, and ask Him to use your situation for good.

Suicide and Crisis Lifeline: (1-800-273-8255) Also: you can dial or text direct to 988

Our ultimate lifeline is God. He loves you. Start by praying and asking Him for help.

65

STEPPING OUT OF YOUR COMFORT ZONE

"Have I not commanded you? Be strong and courageous.
Do not be frightened, and do not be dismayed, for the
Lord your God is with you wherever you go."
Joshua 1:9

Sometimes stepping out of your comfort zone can look like facing a fear, or it can be as simple as wearing something that you wouldn't usually put on. One time when I was doing background acting for a show, I was booked as a passenger on a luxurious cruise ship where I got to wear a cute dress. A few weeks later, they had a "recall" meaning they needed to reshoot more of that scene calling all the people back who were working that day. I was under the assumption I would be wearing the same cute outfit again.

However, when I showed up on set, I was confused as wardrobe handed me a pair of heels, business slacks, and a blazer. It was clear that I would be portraying one of the crew instead. I tried to think of excuses to get out of that terrible uniform, but I couldn't. So, I took the outfit and put it on.

As I was about to go into hair and makeup, I overheard conversation between those in wardrobe as they were also confused why I was wearing a different outfit than last time. It was stated that I had a unique look and that the director had requested me specifically. While I wasn't thrilled about the outfit, I guess it was an honor to be chosen, and I was glad that I had stayed.

Hold on, it quickly got worse. I went into hair and makeup and my hair was put into a slicked back bun. I was not thrilled to say the least to have tons of hairspray and gel combed into my freshly washed hair. Thankfully my skin had cleared up quite a bit, but for months if not weeks before, I would never have agreed to this hairstyle revealing my hormonal acne. The hair and makeup people were actually very sweet and remembered me from last time saying how beautiful my hair was and how they enjoyed curling it last time. They were confused as well why I was portraying a different role for a recall, yet they still complemented my slicked back bun. I was quickly transported back in time to my dance competition days.

Although the day wasn't going the way I had planned, I tried to show gratitude as the outfit was warmer than the initial dress I would have been wearing. And I could wear my Ugg slippers on this cold day. Regardless, I was still cold, tired, and sad about my outfit and hair. I know this sounds overdramatic, but I truly was on the verge of tears and just wanted to go home. At that moment, I looked up from my phone after texting my mom about this horrible day, to being greeted by a hug from two of my friends I saw on set last time! They too were confused why I was playing a different role. We kind of joked about how different it was than last time, but they said it didn't look bad, I just looked more professional. I sent a picture to my mom and my former actress Auntie Susan who said I looked like a model with the sleek hair and business suit.

It ended up being a quick and easy day on set, and the next day I was surprised to have received the coveted SAG voucher while also realizing a higher pay rate than usual. Not to compare the director to God, but the director had called me to do something out of my comfort zone. It certainly wasn't the way I had envisioned, but I had been obedient and reaped the benefits as a result. God does the same calling us to do things that aren't necessarily in our plans but remember, He always has a better plan.

Is there anything you feel like God has been calling you to do lately that is a bit outside of your comfort zone? Pray to Him for the courage to take that "leap of faith" and show obedience by following His will for your life.

ULTIMATE HEALER

"Bless the Lord, O my soul, and forget not all His benefits, who
forgives all your iniquity, who heals all your diseases."
Psalm 103:2-3

This devotional was originally written for myself before the idea came to me to offer it for the benefit of others. Writing has been a form of therapy for me. I have gone from documenting my journey of having horrible hormonal acne and crying every day to having minimal blemishes and becoming much happier.

I've learned through the process that there is always going to be something that we are insecure about. The medication I am currently on is starting to clear my skin, but I have noticed some abnormal water retention accompanying it. This has been very annoying to me because I still eat healthy and work out. If anything, I have been working out more now as my body is no longer limited by an earlier ACL injury.

It seems like a simple formula, eat healthy and workout and you'll be happy with your body, right? But there's so many factors that could affect your body. Is it my cortisol? Is it my hormones? Is it my kidney not filtering properly? Looking up things on the internet and WebMD is great to be informed, but it is easy to go down a rabbit hole looking at all the different symptoms and possibilities where you could just rest and give it to God.

I don't like it when things are out of my control, but we need to remember who is in control. God. He is the ultimate healer and knows all the answers. Your body will also change as you get older, that's just part of life. The sooner you can learn to love your body for what it is right now, the sooner you can live your life well. Realize that God is in control of all things. Remember that God made you and chose your body for you. Be grateful in knowing that truth.

What do you feel is causing you anxiety today that is out of your control?
Pray to God and surrender it to Him.

SECURE AND SINGLE

"For the Lord is good; His steadfast love endures forever,
and His faithfulness to all generations."
Psalm 100:5

I've written in previous entries in this devotional that I never cared what a guy thought about me, but more so, I do like to feel good about myself. I still stand by this statement. However, I'd be lying if I didn't say I care at least a little bit about what people think about me. It's our human nature. We want to be liked whether that be from a significant other or just a friend.

Coming from someone whose love language is words of affirmation, in a prior relationship I always felt secure about myself because of the compliments he would give me. Even with my hormonal acne, he made me feel beautiful. He also complimented my body and liked how athletic and healthy I was as he was someone who also spent many hours working out. I had shared with him about how I struggled with OCD of only eating "clean." Yet, he absolutely loved his desserts, so he even helped me with this as he encouraged me to take at least one bite of his every time we went out to eat.

Now that I'm currently single, it could be easy to catch myself putting extra pressure on my appearance again as I'm still searching for my future partner. I remember many of the guys I liked in high school who didn't reciprocate my feelings then. They came running back when I was in college. Some would say I had a "glow up" but this basically reinstated in my brain that looks do matter. I was the same person in high school that I was in college. Okay maybe I matured some, but I have the same heart. I just looked different. If we are all honest, everyone wants to be the hot ex. I guess in my mind, I think if I backtrack and I am less attractive, I will be unlovable. Hence why I can put so much pressure on myself. Not to mention one of my past relationships claimed that I'd "never find someone like him again," but quite frankly, he's right. I won't. I'll find someone better. And that doesn't always mean just in looks, it can be numerous things that matter, especially how one is valued and treated.

Coming from someone who has been in the dancing, acting, and modeling industry, appearance matters as that is the package of what you have to offer. I often need to remind myself that at the right place and right time, I will find the right guy, one who likes me exactly for how I am, and more importantly for all the other things I have to offer beyond my appearance. I know I am worthy of love. And you are too.

So, in the meantime, be secure in knowing that above all else, God's love "endures forever." He doesn't care about your appearance, your flaws, or any of your other insecurities for that matter. Nothing can make Him stop loving you. If all you have is God, then you have everything you need.

If you are in a time of singleness right now, instead of having anxiety over when and who you're going to marry, I want you to reflect on what God may be teaching you in this season while preparing for that future relationship. Maybe it's like me and learning to be more secure in yourself and loving yourself. Maybe it's to spend more one-on-one time with God. Regardless of what the reason may be, don't rush. You will never get this time again once you are married. Be present and secure in the waiting.

68

GLOW FOR GOD

*"She is more precious than jewels, and nothing
you desire can compare with her."*
Proverbs 3:15

If you've ever been in a jewelry store, you have seen how beautiful the jewels are as they sparkle and shine. Not to mention how much they cost! What if I told you that God says that you are even more precious than one of those jewels?

You are worth so much more. Never doubt yourself for even one minute. And no, I'm not talking about your appearance, I mean truly glowing because you are so on fire for the Lord. The most attractive quality anyone can have is to love Jesus. Makeup comes off, your outward appearance will change as you age, but a heart for the Lord echoes for all eternity.

Be that girl that makes someone question "I don't know what it is about her, but she's different, in a good way." When someone sees you walk by, they aren't attracted to you based on your appearance, but instead by how you carry yourself with confidence knowing that your identity comes from the Lord. Go out and shine even more than any jewel you would find in a jewelry store. God cares about you. He cares so much that He sent His one and only son to die on a cross for your sins to allow you to spend eternity with Him one day. Now that is love and far better than any gemstone or piece of jewelry.

Open your jewelry box or where you keep your favorite pieces of jewelry. Shine a flashlight on the individual pieces. See how they sparkle even more under the lights. That is how God sees you every single day. Now go out and walk with confidence knowing that Jesus walks with you every step of the way.

THANKFUL

"Better is the sight of the eyes than the wandering of the appetite: this also is vanity and a striving after wind."
Ecclesiastes 6:9

Have you ever saved up on purchasing the newest trendy clothes that by the time you buy them, the trend has already switched, and those clothes are no longer in? This can be very similar to women's bodies throughout the years as what was deemed "beautiful" for its time may have changed.

During the Renaissance period, women who had a "soft belly," thicker thighs, and an overall fuller body were seen as beautiful. This extra girth generally meant that they were wealthy as they had the means to eat well. In the early 1900's cinched waists and larger busts were seen as beautiful. In the 20's thin brows, round faces, and hidden curves were trending. In the 50's curves were in. Then it changed in the 60's where petite figures were the goal along with short hair and long bottom lashes. In the 80's, it was permed hair and toned bodies. In the 90's, thin frames and brows were trending again. In the 2000's, abs, spray tans, and low-rise clothes were all the rage. In 2010, thin brows were traded for bold brows with big lips, breast implants, and Brazilian butt lifts (aka BBL's).

Now, in the 2020's, I would say the trends are either thin and toned Pilates girls or athletic women who lift weights with more muscle and curves. I'd say I'm in the middle. One would also say the "clean girl" look is also popular with "glass skin" not wearing much makeup. My hormonal acne was frustrating as I could not achieve this look if I wanted to.

However, there are still people who will wear makeup. There are still people who want either thin or fuller brows. There are definitely people, especially in LA, getting filler, Botox, and plastic surgery. Overall, I feel like society has been more accepting of doing whatever makes you feel most confident. You don't need to always chase the latest trend. You can enhance your natural beauty if that is your desire. However, God made you exactly how you should be, and you shouldn't have to change that. Be thankful for how He took His time creating you.

In the 2nd century BC, the famous statue known as Venus de Milo was crafted presumably as a tribute to Aphrodite, the Greek goddess of love and beauty. It was discovered in 1820 by a Frenchman on the Aegean Island of Melos, and it was missing its arms. It now stands in the Louvre Museum in Paris, and I have been fortunate to have seen it personally. Venus had no arms yet has been considered the "pinnacle of beauty." If anything, this should tell you that your appearance or fitting in with the latest trends shouldn't define how you see yourself as beautiful or not. And as the saying goes, "beauty is in the eye of the beholder."

I want you to stand in front of the mirror and look from head to toe, thanking God for each little detail of how He made you. This is also a good tip for any insecurity. If you continue to feed your brain with these positive affirmations, you will start to believe it and grow to love your body more.

70

ANXIETY

"Do not be anxious about anything, but in everything by prayer and supplication with thanksgiving let your requests be made known to God. And the peace of God, which surpasses all understanding, will guard your hearts and your minds in Christ Jesus."
Philippians 4:6-7

When I was in elementary school, I remembered learning a song to memorize this verse and I am so glad I did, because I often hold this verse close to my heart because I can be a pretty anxious person. When you are feeling anxious, that is a sign it's time to pray. As it says in the verse, whatever you may feel anxious about, pray about it and let your request "be made known to God." Keep praying and surrender it to God, and He will give you peace by calming your mind and heart.

This was one of the verses I had on my mirror to look at every day while struggling with my hormonal acne. And look at what happened! I brought that request to God and prayed day in and day out, and He chose to heal me. Praise the Lord!

However, that doesn't mean all my anxieties have gone away. I still lean on this verse often as I put so much pressure on myself coming out of college feeling like I'm not doing enough. Yet I'm a certified wellness coach, a Pilates instructor, an actor, a model, a content creator for both my own social media while working with specific brands. I also run social media for other companies while creating reels for their marketing. Additionally, I have written two screenplays, and I have now written my first book! My problem is that I have so many interests which I'm told is a good thing, but I just want that one job that I'll do for the rest of my life. I've also been told "it's okay, you're still young," or "life doesn't end when you're 22," or that I'm way ahead of most people for my age right now. However, with social media, of course it's easy to compare yourself to the influencers who are either my age or even younger and already have enough money to buy their own house or drive a boujee car.

I'm definitely a type A personality who wants that perfect scheduled cookie-cutter life where I wish someone or God could just tell me what my job will be, where I'll live, who I'll marry, when and if I'll have kids, etc. All these things give me anxiety looking at the future.

I'll tell you what, we are messy human beings! It's okay to not have everything together. That is when we must trust God most. And in the grand scheme of things, the way to heaven is not based on our resume or the things we've accomplished here on earth, rather, it is based on Christ's resume where He died on the cross for our sins and rose again defeating death. That, in and of itself, is an amazing gift and should be the best way to rid any anxiety by focusing on eternity.

Whatever is causing you anxiety today about your future, pray about it and surrender it to God. Put it in His hands so you can have peace today. Keep praying daily as if it is important to you, it is important to God.

BURDENS

"Cast your burden on the Lord, and He will sustain you."
Psalm 55:22

When I was experiencing my hormonal acne problems, it seemed like that was the only thing on my mind 24/7. I was constantly researching different skincare lines and numerous supplements. In a sense, this was good as I was educating myself, but what I was doing was trying to take control of this issue.

Once I had exhausted all my options, even trying to heal it holistically, I realized that all I could really do was pray. Every day I continued to pray. I just wished God would sit down with me and tell me what to do. Through a lot of prayers, I was directed toward a certain medication. I didn't want to do that originally because I knew it was still a "band aid approach" to what might be a deeper-rooted issue or imbalance. However, do you know what it gave me? It gave me peace. Peace of mind. I took that medication as my last result and truly gave it over to God, trusting His will for my life because I know He is the one in control, not me.

I realize that I cannot be on this medication forever because I might want kids someday. I also realize that when that day comes and I am off the medication, there is a strong possibility the hormonal acne could come back. But I am not going to worry about that because God tells us to not worry about tomorrow. I know it is important to be present each day and show thanks to God for helping me through what was such a burden in my life both physically and emotionally. Not to mention, I came to realize how important my parents were to me during this especially hard time as they held me up in prayer, loved, and supported me. They kept reminding me how much God loved me, and nothing is too small or too big to pray about as God cares about every little detail in our lives. In addition, they helped me financially throughout this journey. There were times I felt like a burden to them as the supplements, skincare, acne facials, and other things were not cheap! I know not everyone has that luxury and I'm so beyond thankful that my parents sacrificed for me to make it work. They showed me that they would do anything for their daughter. I realized through this experience that if they loved their earthly child that much, just think about how much more God loved me and would do that much more!

Whatever may be a burden in your life right now, know that you don't have to go through it alone. Look to the people around you, your family, friends, church community, and even more. Most importantly, you always have a loving God. Give Him your burdens and realize the peace that will fill your heart.

CHANGE

*"Strength and dignity are her clothing, and
she laughs at the time to come."*
Proverbs 31:25

As I have said in this devotional many times, I am a very planned and scheduled person. If I could, I would love to have my entire life mapped out. However, that's just not possible because of a little thing called change. Sometimes it's unexpected. I always thought I'd live in the same city as where I grew up. Afterall, I went to the same high school my mom went to back in the day. I just assumed my future kids would one day go there as well. I don't know, I guess I just never thought anything of it. We are also a family full of lots of traditions which can be good, but I think we need to also form new traditions, new experiences, and become more spontaneous.

Recently, our California family has felt called to move to Tennessee. I love how this devotional has become more of a therapeutic journal that was later meant to encourage others in similar situations. I was encouraged to write down my thoughts and dreams. What started out as a devotional for myself to read, became something that I am proud to share. I cannot wait to read this back in a year from now and see where my life is at because I know God has the wheel. It is important to realize that change doesn't need to be scary, it can be really exciting because of how many possibilities there are in this world and that God has a say in every little decision.

This past April, I graduated from college with goals and dreams. Unfortunately, they included my boyfriend at the time who gave me many false promises including spending my future with him. I believed him and let's just say I didn't really have my own dreams as I was more than willing to support him and all that he desired. Well, that didn't work out and life took a turn causing me to make the hard decision to leave that relationship. This forced me to find myself. I was blessed with new opportunities every week and have been trying out each one presented to me. I am starting to see where my true talents lie and learn which I should begin to spend more time focusing on. I'm excited to see myself in the coming year. Where will I be living? What career will I be pursuing? What new friends will I have made? And potentially, what new relationship might I be in? I know that God will give you back better than what you lost as you trust Him with your future.

Don't let yourself fear change. Moving can be scary, starting a new job can be scary, going on dates and putting yourself out there again can be scary, making new friends can be scary, even your body changing as you get older can be scary. However, I say embrace the change and turn it into a good thing. Don't be scared of the future, for you know we have a good God who already knows what your future holds.

DISTRACTED

"And the Lord God commanded the man, saying, "You
may surely eat of every tree of the garden, but of the tree
of the knowledge of good and evil you shall not eat, for
in the day that you eat of it you shall surely die."
Genesis 2:16-17

In the beginning, God created Adam and Eve and told them that they could eat from any tree they'd like, except for one. In the garden, they were approached by Satan disguised as a snake, tempting them to eat from the forbidden tree. They fell into temptation and ate from the tree. This one act was the beginning of sin entering the world and the downfall of man.

You see, this is what the devil does to us. The devil wants us to look at what we don't have, instead of being grateful for what God has already blessed us with. As I've said in previous devotions, "comparison is the thief of joy." You may seem so completely content one moment with all that you have and then unsatisfied with life the next. One moment you may be fine and then suddenly become distracted by seeing what someone else has as you scroll on Instagram. Perhaps you see something better than what you already have which immediately sends you into the dangerous spiral of jealousy. If we are not careful, the power of envy and jealousy has the ability to destroy.

Don't get distracted by the lies that the devil is putting in your head. He's trying to tell you that you need to own something better than someone else, you need to look better than another, you need to live a better lifestyle than others, etc. Don't listen to him! God has made you exactly as He planned, and He will bless you beyond what you can imagine.

Today, I encourage you to name five things that you see as true blessings in your life. Now go outside and look around. Name another five things that you are grateful for that God has blessed you with that we perhaps take for granted. While you're out, look around and recognize that all those seemingly perfect people you like comparing yourself to on social media aren't at all what most people look like.

74
ASHAMED OF YOUR BODY

"Then the eyes of both were opened, and they knew that they were naked. And they sewed fig leaves together and made themselves loincloths. And they heard the sound of the Lord God walking in the garden in the cool of the day, and the man and his wife hid themselves from the presence of the Lord God among the trees of the garden."
Genesis 3:7-8

When God had created Adam and Eve, they were naked in the garden. It was normal. It wasn't considered strange or weird. In fact, it was a beautiful thing. It was how God designed us to view our bodies. However, as soon as they sinned by eating from the forbidden tree, they instantly felt "naked" and ashamed of their bodies and actions. They felt the need to cover up and hide from God.

The same goes for a common insecurity. Body image has been a focus for decades, but the term "Dysmorphia" has shown up more and more. I would say most people are somewhat ashamed of their bodies and the term dysmorphia is often used. Body Dysmorphic Disorder is a mental condition in which you can't stop thinking about one or more perceived defects or flaws in your appearance. Insecurity is so normalized nowadays that the majority of people have something that they wish could change or become increasingly focused on what they cannot. This is not how God planned for us to live our lives. Now, I'm not saying go run around and be naked, we need to be modest Christians. My point is that insecurity comes from sin. Insecurity may cause you to want to hide from people, run from the world, or even from God. I can relate to that when I was struggling with my hormonal acne. I didn't want to leave the house. I hated staying inside but I was so insecure that my acne was all I could focus on. I needed to give my cares to Jesus. My Aunt Marcia always told me that if I was feeling sorry for myself, go help someone else. That way the focus wasn't on me anymore. And you know what, it works!

Satan is the author of lies and he will do anything and everything to take you away from Christ. But it is important to remember that his lies are not truth! Don't listen to him. Instead open your Bible and listen to what God has to say. He will remind you that you are worthy and beautiful because He is the God of all creation, and you were made in His image.

Look at yourself in the mirror today, unashamed of whatever insecurity you're experiencing, and tell yourself that you are attractive, and back it up with scripture (Psalm 139:14).

SELF-LOVE

"The heart is deceitful above all things, and
desperately sick; who can understand it?"
Jeremiah 17:9

One thing about Satan is he will never directly tell us to worship him. Instead, he will try to make it so that we end up worshipping ourselves and the things of this world instead of worshipping the one and true Lord Jesus Christ.

Satan will do this by tempting you to give into your worldly desires whether that be fame, greed, power, lust, beauty, or a whole host of other distractions. For me, it was beauty. Not that I wanted to worship myself, I still worshipped God above all things, but I was obsessed with the idea of looking a certain way which seemed to take over all of my daily thoughts.

I feel like something that has also been trending lately in this generation is the idea of "self-love." We should love ourselves and yes, it's okay to love yourself the way God made you, but you shouldn't love yourself before or more than God. This is why it says in Jeremiah 17:9 that *"the heart is deceitful."* Don't let your heart be deceived by the devil. I'm sure you've heard the saying "trust your heart" or "trust your gut," but I think we should instead say, "Trust God!" We can't afford to trust our own hearts or thoughts when the devil wants to tell us lies. Instead, we must lean solely on God for wisdom putting Him first in all things.

Today, I want you to love yourself. What does "self-love" look like to you? Maybe it's giving yourself a compliment, perhaps it is thanking God for how He has made you. But then, switch the focus from you, to God, worshipping Him. Maybe that looks like playing one of your favorite Christian worship songs and focusing on Him.

76

A DIVIDED MIND

"And if a house is divided against itself, that
house will not be able to stand."
Mark 3:25

saw this quote one time by Lisa Bevere that said, "Our healing won't come until we allow God to help us change the way we view our bodies." Our thoughts have power. When I was struggling with my hormonal acne, I noticed many people talking about how stress negatively impacts one's body in a multitude of ways. For some, maybe this looks like acne. I remember seeing a video of a girl talking about how things changed when she started to accept the fact that she had acne. She would tell herself that she was still beautiful. Instead of stressing about it, which literally does nothing and often just makes it worse, her skin began to clear. The change came when she switched her mindset of how she viewed her body, specifically her face.

Maybe for some others it's the way they view their body shape. One of my favorite actresses, Madelyn Cline, was open about her past body struggles in an interview. She's similar to me where she used to dance and would also lift weights and do cardio by working out multiple times a day. In the process of that, she was under eating, trying to achieve a body type that she wanted, but it wasn't feasible. Her mom, like mine, was a really big help to her during this difficult time. She would have her stand in front of the mirror with her, making her list specific things she liked about her body. With this repetition of focusing on positive thoughts that she would see in herself; she started to learn that the body type she was going after just wasn't realistic. She wasn't built that way and that was totally fine. She began to learn to love her curves and her hips.

I feel like any girl who has grown up dancing can definitely relate to having body dysmorphia, especially since countless hours were spent staring at themselves in front of the mirror. On top of that, a girl must deal with everything that comes with her monthly menstrual cycle. Some days you might feel bloated or have your face break out as your body experiences its own changes throughout your cycle. One day you like the way you look and the next day you don't. On those tougher days, I really encourage you to not let your mind be divided between positive and negative thoughts, but rather speak only positively to yourself. When you really think about it, it is amazing how God made everything about our bodies so perfectly. We have periods and go through ovulation to ultimately create families. Although we may experience cramps and our bodies tend to change from time to time, remind yourself that God created everything…and He created you exactly the way you were supposed to be made.

There are so many days where my mood just so happens to be determined by how clear my skin is, how my makeup is, how my hair is, etc. If today happens to be one of those days where you're not feeling your best, I want you to come to the Lord in prayer and ask Him to redirect your thoughts in how you are viewing yourself and remember to show gratitude to the Lord for making you. Every day can be a great day, not just a good day.

NOURISH YOUR BODY

"Man shall not live by bread alone, but by every
word that comes from the mouth of God."
Matthew 4:4

Choosing this verse, I thought it was kind of funny, coming from the girl who doesn't eat gluten. However, what the verse is saying is that where it is important to fuel your bodies with eating healthy, it is also important to fuel your soul with God's word.

Something that I think most people, including myself, can be better at is spending more intentional time in the word. Simply by going to church every Sunday, reading a five-minute devotional each morning, saying a prayer before meals, or even listening to worship music in the car is not enough to keep us "fed" by His word. I've actually really enjoyed writing this devotional as it forced me to sit down and have time each day with the Lord, reading scripture, and then reflecting on the word.

Living in California my entire life, I feel like I have always lived a very busy lifestyle, and that shouldn't be an excuse for not carving out time in my day to spend time with God. It's just like they say, you have 24 hours a day, 8 hours for sleep, however many hours for work, surely you can find at least one hour to work out and take care of your body. The same goes with getting in the word! Surely you can find one hour to spend time reading and reflecting on His word and letting Him "speak" to you through the Holy Spirit. Sometimes we are so quick to read that we forget to meditate on the word. Slow down. Enjoy this time with God. Let His word nourish your soul.

I heard about this strategy recently from Pastor Noah Herrin and also read it in his book, "Holy Habits." He lives a very busy and scheduled life. He said that before each thing he has scheduled for that day, he says a prayer before starting the task or activity. This allows him to invite God into every part of his day. Have a workout? Pray before. Have a meeting? Pray before, and so on. It is a great habit to begin and incorporate into your daily life for the rest of your life!

78

CLEANSED

*"And a leper came to him, imploring him, and kneeling said to him,
'If you will, you can make me clean.' Moved with pity, he stretched
out his hand and touched him and said to him, 'I will; be clean.'"*
Mark 1:40-41

In a previous devotion I shared about a woman who bled for many years and who was ostracized from society as a result. Many were concerned that if she came in contact with others that she would cause them to bleed also. This man with leprosy in today's verse had similar experiences as others avoided him thinking that his awful skin condition was contagious as well.

Where all these people wouldn't touch him, Jesus did. The man fell to his knees begging to be cleansed, and he was. Leprosy sounds one hundred times worse than merely having hormonal acne, but for what it was, it was still a hardship that had me "falling on my knees" as well.

When someone "falls on their knees," it's typically a sign of surrender. The realization that "I can't do it on my own, I need God." That is exactly what I did, I gave my hardship to the Lord, and he cleansed me in time. God is a miracle worker and sometimes we need to drop our ego thinking that we can do things ourselves, and instead, come to Him and ask Him to do the things that we cannot.

What have you been doing lately that you've been failing to accomplish by trying to handle it yourself? Have you considered inviting God into the situation to help? There is nothing too big for God that He cannot handle. Pray to Him. Ask Him to help. Sometimes we must wait as God's time is not our time, however, He cares about us, and He definitely hears our prayers!

79
SIN

*"For I do not do the good I want, but the evil I
do not want is what I keep on doing."*
Romans 7:19

Have you ever known something is wrong, but you do it anyways? I like to think of it like this. If you know me, you know I have an extremely sensitive stomach which is why I tend to avoid "trigger foods" that I know don't usually agree with me such as gluten and dairy. Say I was at a Christmas party with a big table of yummy desserts knowing very well that these treats contain gluten and dairy. Yet they look so good that I can't resist. I fall into the temptation of eating the dessert, knowing I'll have to pay the consequences later.

The same things happen with sin. The devil tempts us to make us feel that whatever we know we shouldn't be doing becomes so attractive that we give into the temptation, even though we know we shouldn't. That is sin. And guess what? This breaks God's heart each time we sin. The good news is, He died on the cross for our sins and rose again so that if we believe in Him, we will dwell in Heaven with Him through all eternity. We have a merciful God who paid the ultimate price for our sins and has forgiven us. No sin is too big to not be forgiven. However because we love the Lord, we should want to do our best to live our lives spent pleasing Him. Recognize your sin, ask for forgiveness, and repent! Don't fall into temptation. But if you do, immediately ask for forgiveness and give it to God praying that you will be freed from your sinful actions or thoughts.

Pray this prayer with me today. Dear Lord, please forgive me of my sins. The ones I remember, and the ones I don't. Thank you for loving me even though I am a sinner. I am grateful for your mercy. I want to follow you and bring glory to you. In Jesus name, Amen.

80

WORDS HAVE POWER

*"Let no corrupting talk come out of your mouths, but
only such as is good for building up, as fits the occasion,
that it may give grace to those who hear."*
Ephesians 4:29

Everyone knows that there is just something about kids where they tend to be unfiltered. They may go up to you saying some kind of rude or questionable comment, think nothing of it, then go run off and do a cartwheel. That's because they're still learning.

As adults, I would hope you know the power of your words by now and know what is acceptable to say and what is not. I heard the five-minute rule about critiquing someone's appearance and I absolutely love it. If one of my friends had maybe a lone hair hanging on their sweater, or maybe they had bled through their pants, or they spilled something on their top, these are things that can be fixed within five minutes if you made a comment offering to help. On the other hand, if it is something that a person can't change in five minutes, it should never be commented on. Some examples of these may include topics such as one's weight, their race, gender, or other physical features that come along with how they were born.

I know words have power because I still remember to this day, a girl coming up to me when I was in third grade, telling me that I had small ears and pointing out one of my ear lobes look a little different from the other. This was something that I had never really noticed before that day. I came home worried, asking my mom if something was wrong with me. She calmly reassured me that nothing was wrong with me, I was just born that way. I actually love my tiny ears; I think they're really cute and petite! Plus, ears are something that never stop growing as you get older, so at least I can count on not having overly droopy ears when I'm old.

Not too long ago, I was released from a photoshoot because they didn't realize my ears weren't pierced. I used to have them pierced for a bit, but my one abnormally shaped earlobe caused the earring to get stuck under some skin. This was the skin that grew over my earring during the waiting period of getting my ears pierced. It was excruciatingly painful as a child to get the earring ripped out of my ear. As a result, I never wanted to get my ears pierced again. For dancing, I always wore clip-ons, and in normal day-to-day life, my long hair covers my ears anyway.

I think it's important to embrace your differences and not let anyone's words get to you. Think before you speak and remember that your words hold power. They can have a negative or a positive effect. One never knows how long someone may hold on to that compliment you once gave them. You may also never know how long someone will hold on to the comment you made or the harsh words you once said years ago, even if you may have no recollection of it. An old saying that has been used erroneously for a long time is "Sticks and stones may break my bones, but words will never hurt me." Nothing could be further from the truth! Words can, and do, hurt more than you know.

Ask yourself today, are the words coming out of your mouth pleasing to God? This can be the words you tell yourself or the words you tell others. If they are more negative than positive, try to start making changes. "Do unto others as you would have them do unto you" is famously known as the Golden Rule because no one likes to be hurt. If we take the time to pause, evaluate our words, and think about if they are edifying to God, we will be much more prone to lifting others up than bringing them down.

81
WORTH

"An excellent wife who can find? She is far more precious than jewels."
Proverbs 31:10

One of my biggest insecurities is my big forehead, especially as a dancer who grew up constantly doing slick back hairstyles. Some people might think my hairline just got stretched back over time, but if you see pictures of me from when I was little, you'd know I was born this way. Look at my dad, same forehead. His whole side of the family has the "Bolde forehead." I guess you could say I won the genetic lottery. Not.

However, believe it or not, I wasn't always insecure about my forehead. It wasn't until it was pointed out to me that it was something I should be insecure about. Like I have said in previous devotions, words have a major impact, and people will remember what you said to them (positive or negative) whether you remember saying the words or not.

Back in 2020, I started posting on TikTok and got a few thousand followers. I feel like out of all social media platforms, TikTok has the most brutal comments. I received lots of positive comments about my hair. Many said it was pretty. However, do you know what comment I remember the most? A comment from someone saying my forehead was big. That just goes to show how one negative comment can outweigh all the positives. But we really shouldn't let it. I ended up filtering my comments by typing key words like those replies with the word "forehead" to be filtered out. From then on, I didn't post on TikTok as much. We should never let others have the power to stop us from doing something we love due to a fear of how they would react. Unfortunately, we live in a world now where people can lob verbal bombshells while sitting in the privacy of their living room or bedroom.

A few years later, I was with someone who had his own insecurities. It is silly to think that no one has insecurities because everyone does. Some are just better at hiding them. And others do not allow the insecurities to get the better of them. He had something that he was struggling with and instead of letting it define him, he was very open about it and did something about it. It got me thinking, should I do something about my big forehead? Should I seek help and get surgical hair restoration? Would he still love me? So many irrational thoughts went through my head when I am fairly confident no one really cared or gave it much attention. I am so grateful that I know the Lord and have a good head on my shoulders, and I didn't listen to my inner voice. He never said anything about it, but I was very self-conscious and thankfully I learned to own my big, beautiful forehead.

Don't ever let anyone belittle you, put you down, or try to control you. Generally, that's a warning sign that they are going through their own insecurities. Same with the negative comments from people in the comment section on social media. Hurt people hurt people. As it says in today's verse, you are "far more precious than jewels." Find a partner who will treat you the way you deserve. As for other's comments to you, remember to whom you belong and where your worth comes from. The only one who matters is our great God.

Whether it was on social media or in person, I'm sure you have experienced a negative comment or two in your life. I encourage you to take the time to say a prayer not only forgiving that person, but also praying for whatever they may be going through in their own life that could be causing them to act that way.

82

YOUR SCARS TELL A STORY

*"We rejoice in our sufferings, knowing that suffering
produces endurance, and endurance produces character,
and character produces hope, and hope does not put us to
shame, because God's love has been poured into our hearts
through the Holy Spirit who has been given to us."*
Romans 5:3-5

When I was young, I went on a cruise to the island of Mykonos in Greece. One day I was swimming in the ocean when I came across a sand bar that was out quite a way and I was able to get up and stand up on it. When I wasn't looking, a wave came up from behind me and knocked me over into a big rock. My thigh was instantly gashed, causing me to cry out in pain as I was bleeding. The worst part was getting back into the water because it made it sting even more as I swam back to shore. I made it to the beach and the lifeguard came over and cleaned my wound. Thankfully, I never needed stitches, but I had to apply a cream and wear gauze and a bandage for weeks if not months after. To this day, I still have the scar which comes with its own personal story.

More recently, with my hormonal acne condition, even though I don't really have anymore "active breakouts," I'm still working on my post-acne scarring and pigmentation. Thankfully, this is easier to cover with makeup because I do not have any more textured bumps like I did when my acne was fully blown. However, at the end of the day when I take off my makeup and see my scars, I am reminded of how God got me through an extremely painful time in my life both physically and mentally. God sometimes has us go through times of suffering to not only grow closer to Him, but to also use our stories as a testimony to share with others. These can give great encouragement to those who may be struggling through similar hardships or difficulties but more than anything, we are called to use our past challenges to uplift others and glorify our amazingly faithful God.

Have you ever thought about your testimony? Could you easily share it with someone if you were asked? How has God changed you over the years?

ONE IN CHRIST

*"There is neither Jew nor Greek, there is neither slave nor free,
there is no male and female, for you are all one in Christ Jesus."*
Galatians 3:28

I was so excited to make the high school dance team when I started high school in 9th grade. The team was comprised of Freshmen, Sophomores, Juniors, and Seniors. After practicing each day, we'd all sit in front of the mirrors and do our makeup. I didn't really wear makeup before high school except for mascara. At this time in my life, I was lucky that my skin didn't have any blemishes yet. I remember watching the Seniors do their makeup thinking "Wow! I want to look like them!" This was also 2016 where more full coverage foundation "full glam" looks were in, opposed to the "clean girl" and "glass skin" simple makeup that is popular now in 2024. I asked the Seniors what makeup they used and copied everything they used. I remember walking to class after dance one day with my best friend who I had known since being a toddler when she said, "I miss your freckles." Growing up I always had lots of freckles on my face and body. Once I started using the full coverage foundation, you could hardly see them anymore. There was absolutely no reason for me to be wearing that thick of a foundation as I had no blemishes to cover. If I could go back in time, I would have never done that because not only did we not wash our faces after dance in the morning, but we would also "cake" makeup on, sit throughout the school day, and then dance some more after school still in makeup! Not to mention I'd come home starving and eat dinner right away and then do homework. When I took my makeup off it was often very late when I would then take my shower hours later and then finally go to bed. And guess what? Acne started to appear around the time of my Sophomore or Junior year. Still, to this day, I don't know if the acne back then was from the sweating in the caked-on foundation and lack of skincare education or if I truly had an internal imbalance. I know most recently it was definitely hormonal and an internal issue as I had all the non-comedogenic (doesn't clog pores) skincare and makeup, facials, and my hygiene was on point (definitely not working out and sweating with makeup on anymore!).

Through this very long story, you can see that perhaps my acne back then could have been avoided had I just been confident in my own skin, embracing my freckles. Afterall, some girls nowadays actually use makeup to create faux freckles! Another thing I started doing in high school was getting spray tans for dance competitions. Coming from a family lineage of Swedes and Germans who don't usually tan very easily and being one who likes the way they look with a California tan, I became obsessed with self-tanning and have been doing it ever since. While you can embrace how God made you, at the same time, I think it's also important to do what makes you feel confident. Whatever skin color you have been blessed with, whether you have freckles, no freckles, beauty marks, or other such features, just embrace it and know that you are beautiful just the way God made you and our differences are what makes us special. Ultimately, we were all created equal, and as it says in today's verse, we are "all one in Christ Jesus."

Think today, what is something that makes you different from everyone else? Thank God for spending His time making you just as you were supposed to be.

84

BLESS YOUR HEART

"You have heard that it was said, 'You shall love your neighbor and hate your enemy.' But I say to you, love your enemies and pray for those who persecute you."
Matthew 5:43-44

Have you ever received a negative comment from someone and wanted to have a good comeback? Well, instead of saying something negative back to hurt them, the best thing you can do is have a calm attitude. Don't give the person the satisfaction that they hurt you. They're trying to get a reaction out of you, and by simply being calm and indifferent, that will throw them off. Some of the best "comebacks" can simply be saying with a smile, "I hope you heal," or "I will be praying for you," or as the people in the south often say, "Oh bless your heart." My mom told me from as far back as I can remember to always "kill them with kindness."

I also remember being in an elementary church group that my mom led called "Girls of Grace." I vividly recall her buying each girl a toy sword and gluing on the word "kindness" to each one to teach a lesson. She had the girls stand with their swords drawn and challenged them to always take up their swords and "kill them with kindness" when others were mean or negative. This saying and this visual has stuck with me ever since. I actually went on to win the "kindness award" multiple times during my formative school years. I still consider that to be a great compliment.

As we've discussed in previous devotions about negative comments, people who engage in such belittling verbal attacks could be making harsh remarks due to their own insecurities or jealousies. During such times, as much as we may be hurting from the words said about us, we need to remember who the real enemy is, it's Satan. When we can separate our feelings from the facts, it is easier to be kind and perhaps even have sympathy toward the instigator. We are called to love our neighbor and pray for them, even when it's hard to do so. Jesus came to this earth to show us how to live and how to love. It is our job to try to emulate him as best we can. In so doing, we can go to bed with no regrets as no one can ever say, "Man, I was too kind today!"

Who in your life is a little bit harder to love at the moment? Ask God to help you resemble Christ through your actions treating that person with kindness or at least with an indifferent attitude when they say hurtful things. Don't let their actions get to you or make you do something that would cause you to resent the way you handle that situation.

85

BEAUTIFUL IN ITS TIME

"He has made everything beautiful in its time."
Ecclesiastes 3:11

To whomever is reading this, I am sure you know what it is like to be in a waiting season, whether that be waiting for the job you want, the friendship, the relationship, or if you are like me, the waiting I endured for my skin issues to clear up.

When it comes to waiting, the person I think who emulated patience and has been such a wonderful role model is Madison Prewett Troutt. Perhaps you remember her from being on the 24th season of *The Bachelor* (Peter's season) which premiered in 2020. She was part of the final three and was very open about choosing to wait until marriage to have sex. She became visibly upset that Peter was intimate with the other women during the overnight dates and made the decision to leave during that tenth week.

Since then, she has used her platform having written two books; *Made for This Moment* (2021) and *The Love Everybody Wants* (2023). She even started a podcast called "Stay True" with her husband Grant Troutt. She and Grant got married in 2022 and God blessed her with better than what she lost. Grant was certainly "worth the wait," which she had embroidered on her wedding veil. Now, in 2024, she is pregnant with a little girl! She and Grant also recently moved to Nashville and now attend a church that I visited a few times this past summer. I loved the church and the community so much that my plans include a move to Tennessee in the Spring. I have looked up to Madi as she represents Christ in all that she does. Now, with the possibility of going to the same church, that would be such a full circle moment! Ironically, one other couple that I have followed on social media for more than eight years also attend this church who have set the standard for what I have always wanted in a relationship.

For many years, my dream has been to one day start a family YouTube channel or host a podcast with my future significant other, and just like Madi, I truly believe God will give me far more than I could ever imagine. How cool would it be to not only fulfill that dream, but perhaps "collab" with the people who originally inspired that dream? We will see. I do know for certain that it is all in God's plan and in His timing. I love how this devotional has also functioned like a journal for me, and I will be able to look back on it in the future and see how God worked in my life.

Another thing that resonated with me and caused me to follow Madi was that she too struggled with her skin. And on TV! I can't even imagine. She said on *The Bachelor*, they can film whenever and wherever, so one time, she woke up with a big blemish on her face. "The Bachelor" Instagram site even posted a picture of her with an unedited blemish while Madi posted the same picture having edited it out. She later admitted that her edits were probably not the best decision because it led to a good amount of public scrutiny. Even now during her pregnancy, I love her vulnerability, sharing that her skin has been breaking out. And even so, she has chosen excitement and joy over worrying about skin blemishes as she is beyond thrilled to have her baby girl.

It's so ironic how Madi originally didn't even want to go on *The Bachelor*. It was her friends who signed her up. And having received the call, she prayed about whether she should go on the show or not. Because of her decision to participate, she has been able to show herself as a strong Christ-follower in front of millions of viewers and use her new and current platform to bring people to Jesus. Was the journey hard for Madi? Absolutely. She even talks about going into the bathroom during the show as it was one of the only places where no filming was allowed. It was there that she could find peace and a level of solace amidst the chaos, a chance to write in her journal, and even shed a tear or two from time to time.

God will have us go through difficult times for a reason, but the wait will always be worth it. He will give you back better than you lost. His plans are better than your plans. And everything is beautiful in His time.

How can you show patience today? How do you need to exercise patience in the waiting?

86

WHAT ARE YOU FEEDING YOURSELF?

"And He said to His disciples, "Therefore I tell you, do not be anxious about your life, what you will eat, nor about your body, what you will put on. For life is more than food, and the body more than clothing."
Luke 12:22

When I was in high school, I danced at a studio where a little girl who was part of a rather famous influencer family, came to dance. I started watching "The LaBrant Family" on YouTube. At the time, their channel was called "Cole and Sav." In short, Savannah was brought up in a Christian home, however, when her parents divorced, she did not make the wisest of decisions. She became pregnant in 2012, at the age of 19, by her boyfriend at the time who then left her to raise the baby (Everleigh) on her own. Savannah's sister and her mom were thankfully a big help, but Savannah's life instantly changed. She grew in her faith during this time. In 2016, when Everleigh was only three, they met Cole LaBrant for the first time at "The Grove," a well-known outdoor mall in Los Angeles. He was only 19 at the time. Savannah and Everleigh were on the social media platform musical.ly posting videos as was Cole, which is how they recognized Cole, and he recognized them. Even though Cole is three years younger than Savannah, he thought Savannah was beautiful and had done an amazing job raising Everleigh. There was a definite connection from the beginning. Cole was also brought up in a Christian household, so he and Savannah were able to grow in their faith together as they started dating. They would also post YouTube videos and do long distance dating as Savannah was from California and Cole was from Alabama. They soon got married the next year. Today, they live in Tennessee with five kids, continuing to post YouTube videos, along with posting on other social media platforms. They have written a book, started a Christian app called "Bear Fruit," and ultimately reflect and share Christ through all that they do. Needless to say, this family has been a huge inspiration to me as I want to find my "Cole" one day and be as amazing as Savannah as a mom.

In one of their videos, I love how Savannah exhibited her vulnerability and shared about her body image issues and previous eating disorder. She has always been on the smaller side, but in the beginning of college as she went through some hardships, she would admit she 100% had an eating disorder. She admitted she wasn't very strong in her faith at the time. She would also become upset if her boyfriend paid attention to other girls on social media. She would quickly start comparing herself to those other girls and then feel like she shouldn't eat dinner that night.

Savannah states that growing in her faith was what really helped her relationship with her body. She said, "the more you realize that God designed you in a specific way, and once you see yourself as beautiful, and worthy, and stop comparing yourself to other people and what you see on Instagram, and once you really start digging into your faith, it kind of just goes away."

Prayer and worship and going to church were a big help in this. She says that it's also whatever you're "feeding yourself." Are you always on social media comparing yourself, or are you spending time with God? She says she eventually got to a point where she can go on social media and see those girls and think, "good for her, I'm good looking how I look right now." She has also tried to be super careful with what she says in front of her kids regarding food or body image, trying to set them up for a positive relationship with both.

What are you "feeding" yourself? Are you comparing yourself to others, particularly those on social media? I encourage you this week, at least for one day, take a break from social media and spend more time with God and see how much better you feel.

87

BEING CONSERVATIVE

*"Do not desire her beauty in your heart, and do not let her capture
you with her eyelashes; for the price of a prostitute is only a loaf
of bread, but a married woman hunts down a precious life."*
Proverbs 6:25-26

Being someone who has been a dancer their entire life, I have always been used to wearing "booty shorts" and a sports bra or tank top. Something funny about me is I have always despised wearing jeans. My motto was, "if you can't do a leg hold in it, I'm not wearing it." When I was young, I would go anywhere and everywhere and pose doing a leg hold. Even though I don't do that anymore, I still don't love jeans and would much rather wear a pair of Lululemon leggings. I have also always had long legs where shorts, skirts, or dresses would be "too short" on me, and I would get dress coded at my Christian elementary schools. My favorite story is when I had a Paris themed dance at my dance studio one year and they gave each dancer a pair of sweatpants that said "ooh la la" on the toosh and I wore those to school one day! Yeah, totally dress coded.In my mom's defense, I had a sweatshirt on that covered my toosh the first part of the day and she didn't notice which sweatpants I had on. My school was also very strict about not showing shoulders. I hated t-shirts back then, and I still do now. Each time I wore a tank top to school, I'd have to wear what I called a "shrug." I wasn't a fan of those either. One time, I had a Justice tank-top on with a jacket over it and had planned on keeping the jacket on the whole day, thinking it'd be a fairly chilly day. It ended up being hot, and when I got back to class, my teacher made everyone take their jackets off because she didn't want anyone to pass out because of the heat. I just sat there and didn't listen because I didn't want to take mine off. She then looked at me as did the other students, and my face turned beet red. She took me into the hallway so I could tell her why I couldn't take my jacket off. All ended up being fine, but an embarrassing moment I'll never forget. I preferred the uniforms provided at one of my private schools compared to the other where you could wear whatever you wanted but it had stricter rules. Don't even get me started on P.E. uniforms in elementary school and junior high! Thankfully dance counted as P.E. in high school, and I could wear pretty much whatever I wanted. It was different at this public school, all the way down to the whole dance team wearing bright blue onesies to school with "Saugus Dance" written on our bottoms! Yeah, I have some interesting stories when it comes to school wardrobes.

What I didn't realize is that dress code is there to enforce modesty and not allowing girls becoming a "distraction" to guys. This would make me mad sometimes like, "Why is it on us? Can't guys just control themselves?" In high school, I was "bigger" than I was in college and now. I always ate healthy and worked out, but I took it to the next level working on my body. I had always heard the expression, "If you've got it, flaunt it," and it always made me feel confident when a guy would complement my body. Then I questioned why all the guys were going after me and realized they wanted me for the wrong reasons. Showing too much skin will get you the wrong type of guy and give off the wrong impression of yourself to the guys you want to attract. I'm still not perfect as I sometimes question the line between what is appropriate and what isn't having been exposed to the dance world my whole life. I try to ask myself, "What would Jesus think?" For the most part, I think the outfits I wear in my posts are usually tasteful as that is my goal but my mom still corrects me from time to time.

Evaluate your closet and what you are wearing in your social media posts today. What kind of message are you sending guys?

88

GIVING

"And He answered them, "Whoever has two tunics is to share with
him who has none, and whoever has food is to do likewise.""
Luke 3:11

Lately, I have been going through my closet, getting rid of clothes that I no longer wear. I also helped my mom go through her closet, and we came up with 12 bags of clothes to donate! Not only did it feel good to free up some space in my closet and have everything nice and organized, but I know those clothes are going to someone who may need them more than me. Whatever donation, or community service you do, the intent is not to make you feel good about yourself, it is about helping others and being selfless.

I've participated in tons of community service while growing up. A few examples include volunteering at charity events for the local children's cancer organization and the Boys and Girls Club. I also helped with an annual citywide clean-up campaign, volunteered at the local food pantry, handed out water at the Santa Clarita Marathon, served meals at the senior center on Thanksgiving Day, and so much more. I'd say my favorite out of all of those was the senior center at Thanksgiving because yes, it is nice to have someone bring you a meal, but what the seniors wanted the most was conversation. Bringing a smile to many faces is what truly made their day. I think that's when I first really learned the significance of community service and gave back. When I was in high school, I was involved with Dance Team, National Honor Society, and Key Club where community service was required, and a certain number of hours were needed to fulfill those requirements. However, this was never a problem for me because my dad, who happened to be the school principal, loved encouraging community service for all students. As a result, community service was like second nature to me from a very young age. It was just part of who we were as a family, and I'm grateful that a "giving back" attitude was instilled in me early in life because it is now easy for me to see a need and not hesitate to fill it.

I encourage you to go through your closet today. I'm sure there are clothes you never even touch, let alone wear. Go donate them and make someone's day!

THE STORM

"And when He got into the boat, His disciples followed Him. And
behold, there arose a great storm on the sea, so that the boat was
being swamped by the waves; but he was asleep. And they went and
woke him, saying, "Save us, Lord; we are perishing." And He said
to them, "Why are you afraid, O you of little faith?" Then He rose
and rebuked the winds and the sea, and there was a great calm."
Matthew 8:23-26

Sometimes God will have us in seasons of life where it feels like we are in a "great storm", and we need to rely on Him to get us through. It is important to have faith by focusing on Him, and not the "storm."

There is nothing that God doesn't do without intention. We often go through hardships to either grow in our faith, grow in ourselves, or learn certain lessons. Some common byproducts of those hardships include "hitting rock bottom" or "meeting your breaking point" to start to grow and shine for Jesus. A couple other sayings I've heard is that "diamonds are built under pressure" and "gold is refined by fire." These are great examples of how God takes us through great pains sometimes to prepare us to be our best and to be ready for Kingdom service. God never promises us a life that will be easy. He does, however, promise to never leave our side.

Things can sometimes get a lot harder before they get better. God often uses our tests to bring us closer to Him. I found that out the tough way when dealing with my hormonal acne challenges. When starting a retinol program that increases your skin cell turnover, you may experience a "purge," meaning all that is under the skin needs to come out to be clear. This goes for any acne medication as well. It was frustrating to see worse results than when I started. However, it is critical that you have patience and faith knowing that God will get you through the "storm" and clear skies are on the horizon. Or in this case, clear skin. Had I not gone through those tough times, I would not have depended on the Lord as much as I did and continue to do so. In navigating the storm, my faith grew as well. I have never been closer to God, and that test is definitely now part of my testimony.

Are you currently in a "great storm?" Pray to God to calm the waters and thank Him for never leaving your side. Ask Him for the patience and faith that you will need to travel through tough moments. Be confident in Him and know that only He can and will help you get through.

CORE BELIEFS

"Put on the whole armor of God, that you may be able
to stand against the schemes of the devil."
Ephesians 6:11

When you wake up reach day, the best thing you can put on every morning, better than any designer brand of clothing, is the "whole armor of God." The armor of God is knowing His word. This may look like reading His word, memorizing scripture, and having His word in your heart so that when you are faced with lies the devil is trying to tell you, you can defend yourself with the truth of the Bible.

I'm not sure if you've seen the Disney movie *Inside Out*, but the original came out in 2015, when I was only 13 years old. The sequel came in 2024 when I was 22. I loved that the main character, Riley, was young like me and represented the Gen Z demographic in the first movie. Then the second movie wasn't released for almost ten years and this group was all grown up, just like Riley. The second movie had basic emotions like joy, sadness, anger, disgust, and fear. Intuitively the movie makers added more emotions as it is understood that life gets harder as one matures thus the arrival of more feelings associated with one's existence. "Anxiety" was added as the star of the show as most people can easily relate to feeling this way as they grow older with more responsibilities and pressures added to their lives. I love how this was promoted as a "kids' movie," but I will fully own up to being a 22-year-old who saw it in theaters, tearing up, along with many other Gen Zer's who were posting on TikTok. My mom also loves these movies because she is a counselor and works with students who need help dealing with their emotions. She even bought a stuffed animal version of each emotion for the elementary aged kids to hold as she asks them which emotion they are feeling the most that day.

During *Inside Out 2*, the movie discusses how Riley, along with all of us, has "core beliefs" about themself. For instance, one of Riley's core beliefs was "I'm a good person." However, as the movie progressed with the emotion of anxiety taking over, those core beliefs started to change. Anxiety takes the position of preparing for those "what if" future scenarios, leading to Riley having new core beliefs such as "I'm not good enough." This is just like the lies the devil wants us to believe about ourselves. In times like these, we need to hold onto the truth of what scripture tells us and to whom we belong, not allowing our emotions to get the best of us. When we know scripture, we can hold those anxious thoughts captive and fight them with God's word. As we continue to read, meditate, and memorize scripture we will be quick to fight off our negative thoughts from the lies of Satan.

Take some time to write something about yourself today that you may worry about or may often believe about yourself and then use scripture from the Bible to combat and put a stop to the lie.

ROSES WILT

"Do not lay up for yourselves treasures on earth, where moth
and rust destroy and where thieves break in and steal, but lay
up for yourselves treasures in heaven, where neither moth nor
rust destroys and where thieves do not break in and steal. For
where your treasure is, there your heart will be also."
Matthew 6:19-21

Have you ever had something stolen from you? I remember our family attending a dance banquet at a country club and leaving all my dance stuff in my "dream duffel" in my dad's car because I had to later perform at a dance competition. If you are or have been a dancer reading this, you know what I'm talking about. For those who don't know, it's basically an oversized suitcase. I'm sure the thief thought there would be lots of valuable things in there. Instead, he got a dance costume among many other dance items. My parents tried to comfort me by making light of the situation. They claimed that the joke was on the thief. I am certain that the thief was most likely quite disappointed all he got was ballet shoes, tights, and a leotard!

Not too long after, my mom's car was also vandalized, ironically in the same parking lot! After school one day, my mom and I sadly discovered a broken car window as my elementary school where my mom also worked, shared that same parking lot. Yet again, the thief stole my dance bag, this time a smaller one, that was ready for me to change into my dance clothes after school. When one experiences theft, you feel violated. It is an invasion of privacy. It is an uncomfortable and scary feeling. My parents have always tried to remind me that items can always be replaced, but people cannot. Even though this was another awful experience, everyone was safe. My parents raised me with a Christian worldview so it was easy for me to have a proper perspective knowing that "they're just things" and we can't take them to Heaven with us.

Perhaps for you it isn't something that is a material thing. Maybe it's your appearance. Recently, I received some beautiful roses, and for the first few days, they were stunning to look at every morning. Then, I woke up and saw them a few days later, and they were starting to turn brown and wilt. This is a great reflection of ourselves and our bodies. Beauty fades, and roses wilt. Just like we cannot take material things with us to Heaven, we don't take our exact bodies either. In fact, although our bodies will be recognizable, we will have new bodies in Heaven, free of any imperfections, disease or insecurity! The only thing that does go to Heaven with us is our soul. What is in our heart will remain forever.

Reflect today, are you more caught up in the materialistic things in your life or your physical appearance? Or are you setting those things aside and focusing on your heart and having a relationship with Jesus Christ?

92

BALLERINA BODIES

"I appeal to you therefore, brothers, by the mercies of God, to present
your bodies as a living sacrifice, holy and acceptable to God, which
is your spiritual worship. Do not be conformed to this world, but be
transformed by the renewal of your mind, that by testing you may discern
what is the will of God, what is good and acceptable and perfect."
Romans 12:1-2

I was very fortunate growing up at a dance studio that wasn't like most "cookie-cutter" studios. They welcomed all bodies, and we weren't forced to look the same, especially compared to the pressures known to exist among prestigious ballet companies. I do remember, however, occasionally taking classes outside of my studio where I didn't have such positive experiences. Every dancer knows that ballet is the foundation of technique for any dance style. When you take a class, it is normal for a teacher to correct a student. Oftentimes, the instructor would come around and perhaps correct a certain placement of a body part to make sure the dancer's form is correct. One thing I experienced when I was young was that the teacher would sometimes touch my stomach. This was meant for the sole purpose of having me engage my abdominal muscles. Well, I was young, and I don't think I even knew or understood what abs were! To me, I thought that meant suck it in so I was holding my breath until I literally could have passed out! I guess tapping my stomach was better than some teachers who would say "I can see your lunch!" meaning the stomach was protruding and needed to be sucked in.

Adding to that, ballet attire already causes a high level of vulnerability. Wearing nothing but tights and a leotard standing in front of a mirror while looking at your body for hours causes you to be over-aware of your body. If you're a dancer, you can relate to knowing which areas in the room make you look skinny in the mirror, opposed to other areas. The ideal ballerina body type is very thin and lengthy as you want the lines of each movement to be elongated and pretty. I've actually always had very long legs but have accepted the fact that I will never be "skinny as a twig" because that's just not how my body was made. And you know what? That's okay.

One of the dancers I looked up to while growing up was Sophia Lucia. If you're in the dance world, you know that name! She still holds the Guinness World Record for the most consecutive pirouettes completing 55 turns in tap shoes when she was only ten years old! She was featured in a few episodes of the show *Dance Moms*, as well as winning many dance competitions, and has over a million followers on Instagram. When she was young, she was extremely petite! However, as she got older and went through puberty, she started to develop curves.

More recently, she started a podcast with her best friend Ambry Mehr, called "The Sitch." In one of the episodes, Sophia was very transparent about her struggles with body image. She states, "I think with social media, I've always felt like I've had to live up to my younger self like I must one-up myself. People love to remind me how great I was when I was younger, but it feels sometimes like I'm stuck, like I will never be as skinny, I'll never look that way again, I'll never be that good again, I'll never be all that again." She also opens up about her experience at a prestigious ballet academy where she danced for hours on end. The teacher had her, along with the other students, on a very strict diet with very little calories or protein. It was so strict that there were video cameras set up to make sure the dancers weren't sneaking other food. Sophia even talked about hiding in the bathroom crying because she was so hungry, devouring king-size Kit Kat bars and then hiding them in the trash. She was known as the "curvier ballerina," although this couldn't be further from the truth. Perhaps it just seemed that way opposed to all the other ballerinas who met the ballerina body standard. It comes as no surprise when Sophia left the academy that she began binge eating because she had been under-eating and restricting for so long.

Today, in 2024, she and I are both the same age of 22. She is still a phenomenal dancer and teaches at conventions and studios. She has even said she brings protein bars in her purse sometimes to give to her students to make sure they're eating as she doesn't want any dancer to have to go through what she did as a child. She shares that she is not perfect as she still struggles occasionally with her body image like most people. She has mentioned that she rejects photoshoots or dance videos when she is asked to wear shorts because she worries that her cellulite will be shown. Regardless, if she is a Christian or not, I love how God used her hardships to become an advocate about body image in the dance world. She has been a positive influence on the newer dance generation with the admirable way she works with them today. As it says in today's verse, "be transformed by the renewal of your mind," don't be so caught up in fitting into a certain body standard or mold, for our bodies are "holy and acceptable to God" and we are to be grateful for every part of our bodies.

Dancer or not, I want you to put on your favorite worship song today and dance, thanking God for the body He gave you.

PLANNERS

"The heart of a man plans his way, but the Lord establishes his steps."
Proverbs 16:9

As I have said multiple times throughout this devotional, I am a planner. In fact, today I was looking through some old journals of mine that I wrote over the years and found one from when I was in sixth grade, and I was already scheduling out my days back then! I think it can be wise to plan, and it's not that planning itself is bad, it's when the plans don't involve God when they are in question. We shouldn't trust in our own plans more than we trust in God and His plans for us. The answer to this is not to stop planning, but to stop craving control and invite God into your schedule.

I know for myself, even in my prayers, I have asked God for clarity. I think it is probably better for me to pray for a heart that can put my full trust in Him instead of just praying for clarity. God doesn't want us to feel in control because when we feel in control, we start to trust ourselves instead of Him. Fully trusting God can feel uneasy and out of our comfort zone. Yet, as today's verse says, "the Lord establishes his steps." It can be difficult looking at the future and not knowing what next steps to take, but God knows. He knows it all. Just take it one day at a time and trust Him with tomorrow knowing He wants the very best for us and from us.

Something I've focused on more lately is my breathing. During stressful times, perhaps worrying about the future, focusing on the present and inhaling, count to 3, and exhale. It sounds so simple, but that little action immediately calms me as I can leave the rest to God.

94

HELP

"My help comes from the Lord, who made heaven and earth."
Psalm 121:2

I've never thought of myself as a stubborn person, but I guess sometimes that could be true as I don't always love accepting help. Maybe that's just the only child in me, always being so independent. I remember when I was little, one of my favorite words was "myself!" I remember this especially when buckling my car seat, I always wanted to do it myself and didn't want help. Even as I got older, I never liked group projects in school. I'm a perfectionist and wanted to make sure everything was up to my standards and wanted to do it all myself, guaranteeing a good grade. I was such a perfectionist that when I was little and did sticker books, bless my family for being so patient with me as I would say, "Nooo…. nooo… perfect!" as I aligned the sticker perfectly into its assigned spot.

While it is good to be independent at times, other times we may need to work with others. We may also eventually need help with a project. I know when I was struggling with my hormonal acne, I became good at advocating for myself. I researched so much whether it be non-comedogenic skincare (non-pore clogging), or supplements and diet/lifestyle to heal whatever internal issues were going on. As someone who wasn't the best at science in school, I was now very interested in the human body and how everything has an impact whether it be stress, gut health, liver, kidney, etc. While it's nice to educate yourself, I learned the true meaning of the expression "innocence is bliss." I realized that once you know something, you can't unlearn it. I started to get really bad OCD through all my daily health tasks and trying to achieve clear skin, although with how diligently I stuck to a prescribed routine, it wasn't really working.

On top of that, if you have had an acne issue, you know it's the worst when people start giving you advice. Even though you've already tried everything, done all the research, and knowing what is suggested isn't non-comedogenic skincare, so ultimately, you know it will not work for you. Perhaps they offer information about going on the holistic route. The truth is, whether you use their advice or not, you need to realize they're just trying to help because they care about you, and you should not get offended.

I had tried everything, running myself ragged, having the perfect routines and doing all the right things, but seeing no results. This is not to say that the holistic approach doesn't always work as I've seen others have great results. However, it didn't work for me. It came to a point where my mental health needed to come first. I ended up choosing to seek out my general practitioner and go on the medication she prescribed. Beyond asking the doctor for help, I prayed to God for help that this medication would clear my skin. I almost instantly started seeing the results. I don't believe I mentioned the name earlier in previous devotions, but no gatekeeping here, I went on spironolactone which did wonders for me because my acne was strictly hormonal on the lower half of my face. With that said, it is important to keep in mind that what works for one person may not work for everyone. I do realize that because this is a medication, it could come back whenever I choose to stop taking it. However, I have no idea what will happen. What I do know though is that God will handle my future.

When I finally surrendered to God and asked Him for help, my skin cleared. By simply taking one pill a day versus all the OCD driven wellness habits I was going through each day was nothing short of miraculous. Some of the habits I'll continue doing because I enjoy them and love health and wellness, BUT I'm not going to stress myself out over them. More recently, having achieved clear skin, when a few blemishes randomly pop up, it's hard not to fall back into that "what if it all comes back" mindset and the return of the horrible trauma and PTSD. That can quickly result with falling back into old habits like the restricted eating and being very hard on myself with having the perfect health and wellness routine. In times like these, I need to breathe and remember I'm not the one in control. I've given all that over to God and it was time for me to again, ask Him for help.

Whatever hardship you are currently experiencing, have you prayed to God about it? Ask Him for help.

PATIENCE

"But the fruit of the Spirit is love, joy, peace, patience, kindness, goodness, faithfulness, gentleness, self-control; against such things there is no law."
Galatians 5:22-23

Something I've recently started stressing about is how life would look like when I am married and have kids as opposed to now when I am single. Right now, it is very easy to write out my schedule the day before and check each little thing off the next day.

Recently, I caught a glimpse into what being married and having kids may look like. I still live at home with my parents, and we are in the process of redoing parts of the house, which sometimes comes with my dad asking my mom and I for help with things at the last minute. This is one of my pet peeves because I am totally fine with helping, if I know what time I am needed, in advance. The key phrase is "in advance." Being interrupted in the middle of my workout and throwing off my schedule stresses me out. I am not a spontaneous person.

Bless my mom for being such a "trooper" in her marriage. Watching her, I have seen how to be a future wife and mom. And unfortunately, that comes with dropping what you're doing for the needs of others. A "go with the flow" attitude is what she has learned over the years. It's funny because she claims that she was always an organizer and planner until she had me and saw that I carried that trait even more than her! Along with her patience, she also displays all the fruits of the spirit in her marriage and as a mother. I aspire to be like her one day as she makes even the hard look easy.

Which fruits of the Spirit could you add or improve on today?

96
IT COMES WITH A COST

*"Finally, brothers, whatever is true, whatever is honorable,
whatever is just, whatever is pure, whatever is lovely,
whatever is commendable, if there is any excellence, if there
is anything worthy of praise, think about these things."*
Philippians 4:8

I want you to take a second and think about where you often "pay" your attention. It's called "paying" your attention because everything comes with a cost. If you're "paying" your attention to money, the cost is that it will lead to greed. If you're "paying" your attention to scrolling on social media, the cost of that is comparison. Whatever you spend your time looking at, listening to, or thinking about, it all has an impact on you and determines the kind of person you become.

For me, I struggle with not "paying" attention to what and how much time I spend on social media. It's difficult because a lot of my jobs revolve around social media, so even if I'm on it to post for work, I can easily go down a rabbit hole if something catches my eye. Often, one thing leads to another, and before I know it, I am mindlessly scrolling and feeling less than focused on what's important. It can be a real trap. Luckily, I am disciplined and self-aware so when I realize this, I exit the app and stop.

Today, be mindful of what things you "pay" your attention to and what costs are associated with it. If you're like me and struggle with social media comparison, set a time limit on those apps in your settings. Or if you are willing and want a challenge, delete the app for a week or month and do a social media cleanse and "pay" your attention to God, spending your time in the word instead.

EYES ON GOD

"The eye is the lamp of the body. So, if your eye is
healthy, your whole body will be healthy."
Matthew 6:22

In the Bible, we are called to be a light for others. I remember being in Sunday school when I was little singing the lyrics, "This little light of mine, I'm gonna let it shine… don't let Satan blow it out." There are things or people on this earth that can easily "dim our light." This can come from who we surround ourselves with, or what we are watching, etc.

In today's verse, it talks about our eyes being a "lamp of the body" and if our eyes are healthy, so will our body. Now, that doesn't mean the literal health of your eyes. At one point in my life, I saw the eye doctor and they said one of my eyes was stronger than the other and was overcompensating and could eventually lead me to being cross-eyed. So, I had to wear a single contact lens in the weaker eye, even though I could see fine. Years later, my eyes are fine now, and I don't need to wear that one contact.

How is the health of your eyes? I don't mean this literally. What are you looking at that is impacting the light of your body? Are you looking at things that can dim that light, or things that will make that light brighter, shining for Jesus? Consider "glasses" like reading your Bible. Maybe sometimes your vision is a little blurry, so what do you do? You put on your glasses. When you aren't quite sure what your next steps are, read your Bible for His word is *"a lamp to my feet and a light to my path"* (Psalm 119:105).

Reflect today on where your focus is and redirect your eyes to God.

98
LIGHT OF THE WORLD

"You are the light of the world."
Matthew 5:14

It's interesting looking at all these verses as many of them remind me of worship songs I would sing as I was little in chapel at my private Christian elementary schools. I guess being a dancer, music always helped me memorize things whether it be choreography, or even Bible verses. I remember this song "Here I Am to Worship" with the lyrics, "Light of the world, you stepped down into darkness, opened my eyes, let me see…"

Jesus is a light to this world. He came down from Heaven, leaving His royal throne to take on a human existence on earth, a place filled with sin. Those who chose to follow Him, learned greatly from His ways and could then "see" more clearly how to live. We also can be "lights" to this world. As Christ-followers, we are called to try our best to live like Jesus did, and we do this best by hearing the Word and following its direction. By doing this, non-believers will often question what makes us different, leading us to the opportunity of sharing the gospel with others and being an example of how Christ would want us to live.

My favorite time of year is Christmas. One of the most special moments of the season is when my church sings "Silent Night" at the annual Christmas Eve service. As is our custom, everyone is holding an unlit candle as we start the song. One candle from the pulpit lights two other candles held by ushers. Those two candles each light two more. The flame is passed to every one of the 1,500 guests in the worship center and before the song has concluded, the entire room is illuminated through everyone "passing their light." It's a beautiful ceremony with great meaning. We can do the same thing in everyday life as well. It is amazing how quickly goodness can spread just by one person sharing their light with another.

How can you be a light in someone's life today?

ANSWERED PRAYERS

*"I sought the Lord, and He answered me and
delivered me from all my fears."*
Psalm 34:4

In my family, we have a "blessings jar." It is a ceramic vessel that we deposit slips of paper throughout the year in which we have written down the blessings that happen to occur for our family. We write down anything that we are grateful for that God has blessed us with during the previous 12 months, and then put it in the jar. After Christmas, as we start the New Year, we take time to sit down with each other on the couch, taking turns reading the blessings we have written. This is always such a great way to reflect not only on the fun things we got to do and experience that year, but also think back on the harder times or situations where God was able to answer our prayers. This is the biggest blessing of all because we know God hears and answers our prayers. We are not to fear as we put our full trust and faith in Him.

There is such great power in prayer. Whatever you may be going through, big or small, God wants to help you. Bring it to Him. He will be with you every step of the way. You don't need to fear or be anxious, for He is with you (Isaiah 41:10). He may not always answer your prayers right away, and it might not always be exactly what you asked for, but you need to trust that His plan and His time are always perfect. Isaiah 55:8-9 tells us, *"For my thoughts are not your thoughts, neither are your ways my ways, declares the LORD. For as the heavens are higher than the earth, so are my ways higher than your ways and my thoughts than your thoughts."* His ways are always better than ours. And when He does answer our prayers, make sure you continue to give Him the gratitude He deserves.

Whether it's writing down prayer requests or revisiting them later, it's valuable to look back at the Lord's faithfulness during the year. Checking off answered prayers and acknowledging the Lord for His faithfulness helps us to marvel at His ultimate love for us. You can choose to do a "blessings jar" like our family or find another way to reflect on all the ways that God addresses our needs. Either way, just know that our God is amazing, and He is worthy of all praise.

100
A NEW CREATION

*"Therefore, if anyone is in Christ, he is a new creation. The
old has passed away; behold, the new has come."*
2 Corinthians 5:17

I knew about Christ from an early age as I was raised in a Christian household and regularly went to church. However, it wasn't until I was age 19 that I got baptized. I accepted Christ when I was young, yet I knew it was time to publicly show my obedience to God at that point in my life. I had just experienced a school shooting, life had shut down due to COVID, and my dad underwent emergency heart surgery among other hardships. Despite the gravity of all these events, God was by my side, and He got me through each one.

I don't have the testimony like some may have where they have one big realization that they needed Christ in their life or were "born again" after being baptized. If anything, I feel like I've gone through more since being baptized than I did beforehand believe it or not. So, in a way, my testimony just continues to be built one hardship after another, showing others how God has helped me through every circumstance along the way.

If you feel you are in a place where you are ashamed of your old ways, it is never too late to confess your sins to God, ask for forgiveness, and repent. No sin is too big for God to forgive, and nothing you can do will make Him stop loving you. When you are baptized, it is a great way to share your testimony with others, as a demonstration of your sins being "washed away" thereby becoming a "new creation." When you accept Christ, you have a new identity. You are restored with God. You get a fresh start in life being "born again" and forever changed! Now that's powerful!

If you have already been baptized, I encourage you to reflect on what life events may have added to your testimony since then. If you have not been baptized, there is absolutely no rush as you should do it when you feel like God is calling you to do so. However, I encourage you to consider making that commitment while starting to think about what you would share for your testimony.

101

CONFESS YOUR SINS

"Therefore, confess your sins to one another and pray for one another, that you may be healed. The prayer of a righteous person has great power as it is working."
James 5:16

Have you ever had someone ask how you're doing, and you quickly respond, "I'm fine." We all know this doesn't necessarily mean that all things are going great. Have you had someone ask you how they can pray for you and instead of getting into the big things in your life, you just choose a simple prayer request? Or maybe you're in a Bible study group and everyone confesses things they've been struggling with, and you choose to be non-committal, or you come up with a small request, rather than what's really on your heart. You do this because you're afraid of being judged. Well, guess what? God wants to hear your authentic heart, and He will listen. The same goes for surrounding yourself with the right kind of people. Now I'm not saying that all your sins need to be for all to hear. That's just not realistic. What I am saying is that there should be a greater level of trust in some of your closest friends to assist you in prayer for certain situations.

Although it might be difficult in settings like a Bible study group, you should consider going ahead and opening up and being a little more vulnerable! There is power in prayer, and nobody is going to know what you are going through or what to pray for if you don't share. Along with prayer requests, confess your sins. Don't be afraid of being judged because as Christians, we acknowledge that we are all sinners. Sharing with others may also lead to having an accountability partner as well. Additionally, confessing your sin to God and others will give you relief as you will not have it bottled up anymore allowing you to find peace.

Are you involved at your church? Attending church is wonderful but it is very easy to feel disconnected by just attending on Sundays. It is important to surround yourself with other Christ-followers. Think about joining a weekly small group which will allow you to get to know others more intimately by deepening friendships while growing relationships.

102

MADE ON PURPOSE FOR A PURPOSE

*"For we are His workmanship, created in Christ Jesus for good works,
which God prepared beforehand, that we should walk in them."*
Ephesians 2:10

In 2024, there are approximately 8.2 billion people living here on earth. That is a lot of people! God created, knows, and loves each and every single one, and that includes you. How special is it to know that God took nine months creating you when He only needed six days to create the entire universe? How special is it that He knows exactly how many hairs are on your head and designed you exactly as He intended? How special is it that He knew you before you were in your mother's womb? Do you know that before you were even born, He already knew exactly what your purpose would be here on earth? You are here for a reason! You matter. You are not hidden amongst the others. You are special.

Even if you feel like you don't know what your purpose is yet or you don't have that special testimony, keep trusting God and His timing. Testimonies can develop over time just like mine has and continues to take shape. As you get older, you will also start to find what your purpose is and its value. Even after graduating from college, at age 22, I'm still figuring out my purpose! However, I never doubt that God will use me. I know that some way, somehow, I will be used, and you will as well. He has made everyone for and with a purpose. As Christians, however, our ultimate purpose is to spread the gospel, to love our heavenly Father, and to love others.

Have you thought about your purpose? Job titles don't matter. It is how you use your life's circumstances to share the gospel with others that does.

HEALED

"He himself bore our sins in his body on the tree, that we might die to sin and live to righteousness. By His wounds you have been healed."
1 Peter 2:24

I once heard the following analogy in a recent sermon that I had never heard before and I loved how it captured the idea of Jesus' love for us. Have you ever watched a movie where the guy says, "I love you" first to the girl, and the audience can feel the anxiety as he waits for the girl's response whether she will say it back or not? Well, think of it this way. God died on the cross for our sins because He loves each and every one of us. Whether we choose to have a relationship with Him and love Him back is our choice.

This ultimate love and sacrifice are why we celebrate Easter. "Good Friday" is the day Jesus died on the cross for our sins. I always wondered why do we call that day 'good'? It is because we know what is coming on Sunday morning! He will be raised from the dead and because of this miraculous event, our past, present, and future sins have been forgiven, washed away. All this because we have such a merciful God who will forgive or "heal" us. It is inevitable that we will sin, but we can choose to try our best and repent from those sins. If we repent and believe in the gospel where Jesus died on the cross for our sins, was put in a tomb, and then rose again, we can all one day go live in a heavenly home that has been prepared for us by Jesus. We will live with Him and have eternal life!

Take time today to pray and thank God for His unconditional love by paying the ultimate price and "healing" us from our sins.

COMFORT

"Blessed be the God and Father of our Lord Jesus Christ, the Father of mercies and God of all comfort, who comforts us in all our affliction, so that we may be able to comfort those who are in any affliction, with the comfort with which we ourselves are comforted by God."
2 Corinthians 1:3-4

When you are in the midst of a hardship, go to God for comfort. I remember my mom telling me in 2020, during COVID, that it was a scary time but even more so for non-believers as there was a big sense of the unknown and lots of things changed world-wide all at once. Everyone was quarantined and had to stay inside their homes. People were nervous about a shortage of food and water (and don't forget about the toilet paper!). Jobs were lost and people lost their lives. However, as Christians, we know God is always in control and we must trust Him and find our peace and comfort in Him. Because He comforts us, we then can comfort one another.

One good thing that came out of the COVID days were live streams. My church did a live stream church service every Sunday which also brought lots of encouragement during those difficult times. We also saw some businesses giving out bags of groceries to people in need. It was nice to see a community bond together and support one another. Ironically, a few months prior to COVID, in November of 2019, my community of Santa Clarita also suffered the trauma of a tragic school shooting at my high school. The whole community, including students and parents from all the schools in the valley came together for a moving memorial at Central Park. Yet, what meant even more to me was that the night of the shooting, many churches throughout the valley opened for services, along with prayers, and support.

As I have said in previous devotions, this is why a community is needed. It is important to find a church, and from there, find a group of people whom you can lean on during hard times, and in return, support them during their hardships. God didn't call us to do life alone. I know for me, during my skin journey, it was natural for me to take comfort in God along with my parents, but I didn't want anyone else to see me because I was embarrassed and didn't want to be vulnerable about what I was going through. Know that it can be scary at first, but sharing with those around you can strengthen relationships, especially for future times of difficulty when you may need to lean on one another. I was glad that I talked to my friends as they were incredibly supportive and helped me get through this very difficult time in my life.

Because we seek comfort from God, we can comfort others. Is there anyone in your life right now that you know is going through a difficult time? I encourage you to either privately pray for them, reach out to them, and/or even pray with them and ask if there's anything that you can specifically do for them.

105
THE HARVEST WILL COME

*"And let us not grow weary of doing good, for in due
season we will reap, if we do not give up."*
Galatians 6:9

We have all probably asked the question, "Why do bad things happen to good people?" Over the past few years specifically, it felt like my family and I were undergoing continual hardships without knowing or fully understanding the reason why. What we do know, however, is God got us through each and every one. When I was experiencing my terrible acne, it really took a toll on my mental health and all I could keep thinking about was, "Why God?" "Am I being punished?" My mom would tell me, "No, you're not being punished, but God is wanting you to rely on Him." Sometimes, we don't know why things happen to us until much later. All God asks of us is to keep our faith in Him, continue to pray, and to get up each day trusting that He will be our guide. Don't give up. Trust that He will get you through that difficult season. Trust His plan and His perfect timing. Know that you will reap a harvest at the end. Even if what is at the very end isn't on earth, you are assured that you will spend eternity in heaven IF you accept and believe that Christ died for your sins.

I believe that God does everything for a reason and with a purpose. I have come to realize that had I not struggled with my skin issues, I would have never written this devotional with a chance to impact others, and you wouldn't be reading this. There are times when Satan is going to want to knock you down, but don't lose your faith in God and don't stop doing good works. The worst thing you can do is become "hard hearted" because of the cards you have been dealt. Ultimately, through our struggles we become stronger and more resilient and hopefully we will be used by God to help others as a result of them.

Whatever you may be going through right now, pray to God for the strength to not give up while believing that the "harvest" will come. It may not look exactly like you had imagined but God does want the very best for you and we need to trust in that truth.

106

HAPPINESS IS A MINDSET

"Joy comes with the morning."
Psalm 30:5

Have you ever had a bad day and you're around someone so happy that it annoys you? Or for me, my dad is one hundred percent a morning person. Now, I'm not saying I'm not, I'll get up early, but it takes me a little time to function when he is already shouting "It's gonna be the best day ever!" That made me think, what if happiness is really just a mindset?

Recently, one of my favorite things to do in the morning has been going outside on the balcony and getting some sunshine even if it's just for a few minutes. This is not only good for one's circadian rhythm, but it starts the day off right being outside around nature, feeling the fresh morning air, and just thanking God for another day. I often will do some morning stretches as well while listening to worship music outside. One of my favorites is "Good Day" by Forrest Frank. No matter how you woke up that morning, it's a reminder that you can make it a good day.

It's also kind of like how one may feel when they need to work out but doesn't want to. Yes, it takes discipline, but you can switch your mindset by tricking yourself that you are about to have the best workout ever and you are excited and grateful you get to move your body. I always love the "get to" mindset where you shift from "I have to," to "I get to." I get to wake up early. I get to work out. I get to go to work and I get to earn some money.

I know several times this year when I was struggling with my complexion, I would get stressed about things as little as going out with friends or to any event where I needed to put makeup on. I knew that I would want to cover up my acne, but I still felt like makeup made it worse even though it was non-comedogenic (doesn't clog pores). Since I have been on medication, it is evident that my acne was clearly internal because I'm using all the same products as before and my skin is fine. I think perspective is everything and all of those times when I was stressed about my skin while going out, I should have had the mindset "I get to" go out with friends, "I get to" do this for work. At times, I wish I had a 9-5 job, but often when I tell people about my freelance opportunities (modeling wedding dresses, acting on set, creating reels for companies, or running their Instagrams), most people say they would love to do those things.

When I was struggling with my skin, one of my favorite Youtuber's who I mentioned in a previous devotional, Mary Sergi, was also having skin issues. However, her perspective would be, "My skin's breaking out, but it's literally fine. It's normal." I think for any difficult situation you are going through, the "it's fine" mindset is also great to have because you know it's in God's hands.

I've had people intentionally hurt me by claiming that my family and I are "fake." They usually don't know us well enough. We really do try to be happy people who are able to find the positive side of even some of the most negative of situations. Even in times of difficulty, we see our blessings. I've also had a lot of people think my life is "perfect" mostly due to what they've seen on social media, yet they have had no idea what I have gone through and how hard this past year, in particular, has really been for me. But when you have God, you have everything you need. Our true joy and happiness truly only come from having Christ in our lives.

Today, let "joy come in the morning" by stepping outside thanking God for another day praying to Him. And if you want, put on the song "Good Day" by Forrest Frank and dance. Let this set the tone for your day.

107

FOR THE GLORY OF GOD

"So, whether you eat or drink, or whatever
you do, do all to the glory of God."
1 Corinthians 10:31

We have all heard the cliche "do what makes you happy," but what if I told you that's not what the Bible tells us to do? We are called to do what glorifies the Lord. Sometimes, being a Christian can actually look like the opposite of being happy. Hardships are inevitable and the devil will try to attack you and destroy your relationship with God. God doesn't promise us that life will be easy, but He does promise that He will help you through any trials that come your way. His priority for our lives is not happiness, but holiness. When you follow Christ, you will become more like Him, and from that, you will discover true joy and happiness.

I once saw this quote that said, "joy is the deep down settled confidence that God is in control of every detail of our life." Our God is omniscient (all knowing), omnipresent (everywhere), omnipotent (all powerful), and imminent (God is with you). This year was a lot for me as I struggled with my acne issues, a torn ACL, a toxic relationship, trying to figure out what I wanted to do as a career, and contemplating a potential move across the country. But knowing that God is in control of it all brought me peace and joy amongst difficult times. And from those times, especially with my skin, I wrote this devotion to help me but not for my glory. I wrote it for God's glory.

What in your life makes you happy? Is it glorifying the Lord or is it there just to bring you pleasure? Make sure all that you do is bringing glory to God and not yourself.

108
FAITH = CONSISTENCY

*"Then He touched their eyes, saying, 'According
to your faith be it done to you.'"*
Matthew 9:29

In the Bible, Jesus performed many miracles. In Matthew 9:27-31, we see Jesus heal two blind men because of their faith in Him. When I was struggling with my acne, I prayed every night that He would heal my skin. However, something I've realized is you can't just pray and say the words. Do you believe what you are saying? Do you believe that He will heal you? To have faith in the Lord is to consistently believe in Him.

In the meantime, when waiting for a prayer to be answered, control what you can control like meditating on His word day and night. There are some things that are just out of our control and are not consistent. For instance, as my skin was healing, there would be some days when my skin was getting better, and then the next day there was a new blemish which would lead me to spiraling and thinking that it would all come back again. This then led me to OCD tendencies I had experienced before while trying to clear my skin. Sadly, I wouldn't stop until my skin was consistently clear.

In life, there are things we can be consistent with like our workouts, skincare, etc., but there's some things that are simply out of our control. That's where our faith steps in. Have consistent faith in the Lord and keep praying and believing He will heal you or lead you out of whatever hardship you are enduring.

Today, when you pray, don't just go through the motions. Really think about each word that you say and believe them. It is also important to know that God does hear us. He does and will answer prayer. However, it is important to remember that He not always answers us the way we want, and His timing may take much longer than we desire. But the one thing we need to remember is to trust Him having full assurance that He does hear and will answer our prayers.

109

FINDING A PARTNER

"Then the Lord God said, "It is not good that the man should be alone; I will make him a helper fit for him.""
Genesis 2:18

I have said in previous devotions that when undergoing hardships, you shouldn't have to carry the weight alone. You have God and you should surround yourself in a community of other Christians. The same goes when looking for a life partner. As you feel more confident in yourself and love God more than anyone, you may want to share that love with someone else. As we read in Genesis, God created Eve as a helper for Adam. Now ladies, I am sure you have heard the expression that we are the "missing rib." Even so, we shouldn't necessarily be the ones looking for a husband. Instead, we should trust God's timing that He will bring the right guy into our lives at the right time. That's not to say that there won't be guys sent into your life with other purposes. Perhaps they may be sent to you for "a season" to teach you a lesson, to help you learn more about yourself, to help you get closer to God, or to help you learn what you do want or don't want in a future partner.

When dating a guy, it's important to ask yourself what kind of husband he will be. Does he just like you for your appearance? Does he want you for the wrong reasons? Does he respect you? Does he love Christ even more than he loves you? One of the best pieces of advice I had ever heard was to ask yourself if you would let your future daughter date the guy you're going out with. If that question rubs you the wrong way, he's probably not the one. My momma always told me to choose a Christian man and make certain that you choose the nice guy with the kind heart because he's going to be the one who will love you the most and treat not only you the best, but your future kids as well.

While I think finding the right person is important, it's also important to be the right person. Check yourself and ask yourself if you are marriage material and if you resemble the characteristics of a "Proverbs 31" woman.

110
FOOD FREEDOM

"Everything that lives and moves about will be food for you. Just as I gave you the green plants, I now give you everything."
Genesis 9:3

I have been journaling for about four years, and during that time, in each journal, I have also written down what I ate that day. This was a strategy that I used when I was trying to determine which foods hurt my stomach. I learned from this that cutting out dairy and gluten led to a lot less inflammation in my body. When you find out what foods your body tolerates well, that's great! Stick with them. However, I'll admit for at least the last three years, I pretty much ate the same thing every day starting with a bowl of protein oatmeal (Equip protein powder is my favorite, clean ingredients), a protein bar for lunch (Rawr bars are awesome, clean ingredients and they actually have Bible verses written on each bar), a beef stick for a snack (Chomps are great, clean ingredients) with some fruit (I love all fruit!), and for dinner, organic chicken (cooked in avocado oil spray), broccoli, and either a purple potato or jasmine rice. This doesn't even include my morning celery juice, aloe shot, herbal teas, and 80-120oz of water every day.

While I do have some legit food sensitivities, just as today's verse says, there are still so many options for food that I can eat. I think as I've gotten used to what works for me, I get nervous to branch out wondering what might break me out, make me bloat, hurt my stomach, gain weight, etc. Me taking such an interest in the body this year, I learned that we need diversity in our diet for gut health!

I have an internal checklist of what I eat each day, some days I would get frustrated at myself why I'm extra hungry when I eat the same thing every day and my metabolism should be used to it. The thing about being a woman is, our hormones fluctuate throughout our cycle and there are certain times of the month where we may need more food. I have learned that's okay! Everyone must eat. Some may think that you should skip breakfast the next day if you have gone out the night before or during the holidays. You need to eat! And fun fact, eating breakfast within the first hour of waking before coffee is vital for healthy and balanced hormones.

I don't see a problem with keeping track of what you eat each day for the sole purpose of finding out what foods agree with you or not. However, if it becomes an obsession or a problem for your mental health, that's when you need to stop. During my freshmen year of college, I downloaded an app to log my calories, and I would be happy if I ate under 900 calories that day. On top of that I was dancing, weighing myself every day, and chugging a ton of water hoping to make myself throw up. I wasn't in a good mental state. I was also lonely and in a dorm by myself because of COVID. Luckily, I realized that I needed to delete the app because I knew this was not a healthy way to live. Fortunately, this all-consuming focus on eating turned into a positive thing for me as it made me more health conscious while allowing me to discover which foods do or don't work for me (I have since cut out dairy and gluten). I do find it funny though how most people gain weight in college. I am fitter than I was in high school because I have been more mindful of what I eat. I have always danced, but I also started incorporating my own workout routine as well.

There's a lot of different kinds of eating disorders nowadays. I would say the one I still struggle with is orthorexia, "an obsession with eating foods that one considers healthy." Although I have good intentions, the extra stress with how expensive this lifestyle is realized with the escalated prices at any grocery store. Something that I joke about is what a bland cook I will be as a wife. I don't even season my chicken! With that said, I have met some guys who also are anti-seed oils so there's hope! Haha. It worries me that I will have to make food for others beyond myself. My guess is that my future husband and my future kids aren't going to want to eat the same thing every day or what I want to eat. Clearly, I am not ready to get married anytime soon. However, now that I think of it, my dad has similar tendencies. I'm pretty sure he eats only a bite of banana, a Caesar salad, a power-bar, chicken, sugar-free popsicles and iced tea every day and is quite content with that way of eating. As for my mom, bless her heart, she's definitely an "almond mom" who could have a handful of almonds and be satisfied. I've been trying to get her to eat more protein lately. She always said that if she could just take a pill for a meal, she would. Spending an hour to cook something that is consumed in ten minutes and then cleaning up the kitchen isn't worth the work. I don't blame her as we all have certain food routines and there are only three of us. I think it's funny when men ask women if they can cook. Like yeah, I can read directions and follow them, it's not hard. It can be stressful looking at the future wondering if your partner will have the same food preferences as you do. I have observed relationships where the wife is more health conscious than the husband and they are able to make it work. I think communication is everything in a relationship and trusting God and knowing that He will give you the right person at the right time.

I challenge myself, and you, to look up a new recipe this week and try it as God has blessed us with such a wide variety of choices! If you are ever having anxiety over food, I encourage you to look at what you are about to eat and thank God for the food as nourishment. Have a heart of gratitude as some don't readily have access to food as others.

GOD FIRST

"But seek first the kingdom of God and His righteousness,
and all these things will be added to you."
Matthew 6:33

Have you ever taken a group photo and you check it out afterwards and what is the first thing you do? You look for yourself. You want to see how you look. You don't really pay much attention to others in the photo. If you're looking good, all is right with the world. I've been guilty of this several times, especially when it comes to choosing the family Christmas card photo! The truth is, we as human beings are born sinners and can be very selfish.

God isn't selfish, but He is unwilling to share your heart with anyone or anything else. Meaning, God should always come first in your life whether that be while considering your friends, significant other, family, work, sports, hobbies, or any number of other things that tend to take up our time. If you ever hear someone say that they "don't have time for God," that is a complete lie because you make time for what is important to you. That goes for relationships too! And here is a little dating tip, if you mean something to someone, they'll make an effort. They will answer the text. Even if it takes canceling their own plans or rearranging their schedule, they will show consideration. They will acknowledge their commitment to you. You should do the same for them in return, and we should all do this for God. Even if it's just 15 minutes, take time to read His word and be "fed" each day, rather than just coming to church once a week. God has so much to share with us and He wants your attention because He loves you.

In what way can you be more selfless today and how can you intentionally carve out time each day to spend with God? I highly suggest that you plan when you're going to do it ahead of time or else it can be easy for the day to slip on by. It's not that you "didn't have time," it's that you "didn't make time."

112

UNWAVERING FAITH

"Count it all joy, my brothers, when you meet trials of various kinds, for you know that the testing of your faith produces steadfastness. And let steadfastness have its full effect, that you may be perfect and complete, lacking in nothing."
James 1:2-4

When I was struggling with my acne issues, it truly seemed like it would last forever. It was a real testing of my faith, and it took a genuine belief in God's timing and His ability to heal my condition. It's because of those beliefs that allow me to see a healing process that has begun.

In today's verse, it says to "count it all joy" no matter what trial we are enduring at the moment. Sometimes, it's hard to find joy in our circumstances. It doesn't mean that you're happy about what you're going through. What it means is that we find joy in knowing that God is on His throne and orchestrating something in our life that we will be able to cling to in the future. Everything has its reason.

Because of your unwavering faith, you have hope for that future. You find peace being confident that God knows and cares about everything you are going through or may be worried about. Even if you cannot fathom how you are going to get out of a situation, be assured that God knows. He knows the how and the when. He also knows the why.

My mom always said that things come and go in life, and nothing lasts forever. But she reminds me that on earth the only things that can never be taken away are a person's education (diploma, degree, awards, accolades, etc.) and most importantly, one's faith. Faith is everything. It's the most essential thing because if you have faith in the Lord and in His plan, you lack nothing and you can rest in the fact that you are "perfect and complete."

How is God testing your faith today? Whatever trial you may be experiencing, remember it is in His hands, and He cares about you and your faith will get you through.

113
GOOD NEWS

"He will wipe away every tear from their eyes, and death shall be no more, neither shall there be mourning, nor crying, nor pain anymore, for the former things have passed away." And He who was seated on the throne said, "Behold, I am making all things new." He also said, "Write this down, for these words are trustworthy and true."
Revelation 21:4-5

The first part of this year, I think I cried almost every day whether it was about my skin or about a confusing relationship. FYI, crying every day is not healthy! It's okay to cry every now and again as it releases oxytocin and is good to get your feelings out. God knows exactly how many tears you've cried and in today's verse, we can rest on the encouragement that one day, God will wipe away every tear from our eyes and there will be no more crying. There will be no more death, mourning, crying, or pain.

Oftentimes, I miss my youth where I had no worries without a care in the world. Even as I grew older, all I really had to focus on was dance and school. Now being out of college and in the "real world," it seems like life only gets harder as one gets older. One of my favorite movies is the movie *Barbie*, and I relate with how Barbie realizes that everything is much harder or imperfect (exemplified with cellulite and acne in the movie) in the "real world" as opposed to "Barbie Land" (like being a kid with nothing to worry about). Well, what if I told you there's a place that is even better than Barbie Land? It's called Heaven.

The struggles of this earth aren't forever, and because of the gospel, we have the opportunity to go to Heaven one day where all things will be made new. If we believe in the gospel, that "Christ died for our sins in accordance with the Scriptures, that He was buried, that He was raised on the third day in accordance with the Scriptures," (1 Corinthians 15:3-4) we will go to Heaven. And in today's verse, God claims this to be true. It is our job here on earth to share this good news with others!

I heard this analogy one time at Way Church in Nashville, and I really liked it. The current church building is very small. It is rented and there are lots of people attending to the point that there are now three services! And the church has only been around for a little over a year! The Pastor said, what if someone was willing to give our church a check to build a new building but didn't tell us and just assumed we would somehow find out that they have that check for us? Why would someone withhold such great news to themselves? Same goes for the gospel. We need to share it with others! After all, it seems like there is always such negative news nowadays, people could use some positivity! That is why the gospel is often referred to as "The Good News."

One of the positives from social media is the fact that the gospel can be spread a lot more quickly now than ever before. The gospel may be shared by something that is posted, or in person when the Holy Spirit inside of you calls you to take action and speak to someone by sharing the gospel. It may seem a little scary, but it is even scarier if that person doesn't know about Jesus. Step out of your comfort zone. You could change someone's life. Even if that person rejects the good news, you were obedient and tried. You just never know what may result as you planted a seed in someone's life.

114

SAVED THROUGH FAITH

"For by grace you have been saved through faith. And that is not your own doing; it is the gift of God, not a result of works, so that no one may boast.
Ephesians 2:8-9

Often, people think we need to do good works to get into Heaven. While we should try our best to repent from our sins and live our lives like Jesus Christ, what we do here on earth does not define us or impact our eternity. That is solely based on where our faith lies. If we accept Christ as our Lord and Savior and believe the gospel… that he was born of a virgin birth, that He lived a spotless life, was crucified for our transgressions, and was raised on the third day, we will go to Heaven where we will dwell for all of eternity.

It doesn't matter how many good deeds or community service projects you complete, what you do for work, what your job title is, how much money you earn, how many followers you have, how attractive you may be, etc. We are called to not get caught up in the things of this world because in the grand scheme of things, none of those things matter. One day, we will all stand in judgment and the only thing that will matter is whether or not you have built your relationship with Jesus Christ and if your faith is in Him.

I remember when I was little, I would often check in with my mom asking, "I'm going to Heaven, right?" just for confirmation. She reassured me reminding me that I believed in the gospel. She also shared that my continual asking showed just how much I cared. We are to have a healthy fear and reverence for God. As we mature in Christ and we follow Jesus, we are confident that our eternity lies in heaven where He has gone to prepare a place for us.

Ask yourself, if you were to die today, would God know you? Do you have a relationship with Him? It is one thing to say you believe in God, but it is another to actively spend time reading His word and "talking" to Him through prayer. Where is your commitment?

115

YOU HAVE A GIFT

"For as in one body we have many members, and the members do not all have the same function, so we, though many, are one body in Christ, and individually members one of another."
Romans 12:4-5

Along with the gift of the gospel, He has given each of us different gifts while we walk on this earth. These can be talents and skills in a sport, in work, in a hobby, or many other things that occupy our time. Growing up, I knew one of my talents that God had blessed me with was in dance. Whatever our gifts may be, we are to honor Him through each and bring glory to His name as an end result.

I knew right away that I had found the right church when I felt like I was at a concert during worship. Many people were dancing while they were singing praises. They were not dancing to the extent that I would at a dance class, but at least they were jumping up and down, moving, and letting the music move them. The church I grew up in was filled with people mostly just standing as they sang while just a few might feel inclined to raise their hands.

Now, there's no right or wrong between the two. People worship in many ways. For me, as a dancer, when I hear music, I need to move or else I'll get bored. I remember when I used to take singing lessons as a young girl, I would just be standing there, and I would get bored, and I would yawn. A lot! And the same thing would happen in church. At one of my private Christian elementary schools, we had a Christmas concert where the kids would sing for the friends and family who came to watch, and we have a video of me yawning eleven times throughout the whole showcase!

Along with God giving us all unique gifts, He's made each of our bodies different. In dance, there are many teams that have a "cookie cutter" look as they always appear the same. In dance, this can help make the dance look cleaner if everyone is the same size and height. Some teams may even have close to the same hair color and/or skin tone. For me, I was lucky to have coaches who prided themselves on not having a copy and paste kind of team. Instead, they would rather have more of a diverse team representing the differences that God has given each one of us. And we still were National Champions every year in both high school and college.

At CBU where I attended college, we had a Christian focus. I loved our motto, "PGS." It stood for Passion, God, and Success. It always made sense to me as I truly believe that God gives us gifts and talents that oftentimes end in success which is a byproduct of following the Lord's leading.

What gift(s) has God blessed you with? How can you use them to honor Him?

116
CHILDREN ARE A GIFT

"Behold, children are a heritage from the Lord,
the fruit of the womb a reward."
Psalm 127:3

In addition to the gospel and our individual talents, children are also a gift from the Lord. This may sound surprising, but I don't put that much emphasis on looks in a relationship. This is going to sound vain, because I do care when I think about my future kids and what they might look like. I'm not even kidding, several years ago I genuinely asked if it is okay to spray tan a baby. I know, don't judge me and yeah, not happening. The thing is, just as God loves us, we should love our children unconditionally.

A lot of the time, parents want to live vicariously through their children. For the most part, I've seen this especially with moms. My mom didn't do this, but I've seen other moms force their kids into pageants, cheer, dance, gymnastics, etc. I chose dance because that's what I loved, not because my mom pushed me into it or because she had been a dancer. My mom played youth softball and ran track in college which couldn't have been farther from dance.

I think a lot of this stems from a parent's own insecurities. Maybe they were embarrassed how they looked when they were younger, so they want to make sure their own kids always look cute. Maybe they were bullied and want to make sure their kids don't ever experience something like that and are able to stand up and defend themselves. I know for me; I don't want to project my insecurities onto my child. However, I have struggled a lot with looks and body image. I truly want my child to be secure in his or her appearance. I think these are some valid reasons why it is important to be confident in yourself first, by knowing that you are a child of God, before having kids or getting into a relationship.

I truly do think children are such a blessing. I have always loved being around kids, hence why I originally majored in elementary education to become a teacher. This was before I switched my major to film production as I got more into acting. However, as I matured, I am experiencing the present time where some of my friends are getting married and having babies. I must say that the thought of having my own children seems a bit daunting. I'm nowhere near ready for that now. However, I know that I will be someday and that I'll eventually want children in the future.

As a Christ-follower and a believer of God's word, I one hundred percent would never get an abortion. Every baby is a blessing and that is a loss of a precious life. I would have that baby, and no matter how it looks, I am loving it with all my heart, just as God loves us.

Whether you have children or not, think about your own insecurities and what you could be reflecting on your children or future children. Pray for God's guidance towards loving yourself more so that you can love others. It's just like an oxygen mask falling from inside a plane or putting your life jacket on while on a cruise. They always instruct you to put yours on before helping others. While there are times we should put others before ourselves, there are also times where we need to put ourselves first so that we can help others. This can even look like loving ourselves to allow us to love others or being confident in ourselves so that we can have kids and not put our own insecurities on them.

117

HIS NEVER-ENDING LOVE & MERCY

*"The steadfast love of the Lord never ceases; His mercies never come
to an end; they are new every morning; great is your faithfulness."*
Lamentations 3:22-23

When a relationship comes to an end, maybe you miss feeling loved and wonder if you'll ever find that again. Well, what if I told you that God will give you back better than what you lost? That love will find you again, but during the waiting, remember that the Lord's love for us will never end. Whether it be relationships or friendships, have you ever noticed that the word "friend" has "end" in it. God's love, however, will never end and He will never stop loving you.

Even when you mess up, which is a given as we were all born sinners, there is nothing so bad that you can do that will make God stop loving you. The same goes for His mercy. There is nothing so bad that you can do that would cause God to turn His back on you. That doesn't mean we should go about our daily lives sinning non-stop. We should still acknowledge our sin and repent, but in times where we mess up, His mercy is there for us. We don't deserve it, but that is just how gracious our Heavenly Father is.

When I think of sin, I always thought more of the ten commandments and the bigger sins one could commit. The truth is a sin is a sin whether it be big or small. Even the thoughts we have when we critique our bodies that God masterfully created, is a sin. It is important to ask for forgiveness as we recognize where we fall short.

What sins do you need to pray to God and ask for forgiveness for today?
Thank Him for forgiving you for that sin while also thanking Him for His
never-ending love and grace.

118

A GOOD WORD

*"Anxiety in a man's heart weighs him down,
but a good word makes him glad."*
Proverbs 12:25

I mentioned this before in previous devotions, but whenever you are feeling anxious, that is a sign for you to come to God and pray. Sadly, anxiety tends to increase as one gets older. I don't remember really having much anxiety as a kid, but the older I got, the more I internalized stress and uneasiness.

I have always encouraged others to write verses on a mirror to look at when faced with the lies of the devil that he tries to tell you. The same goes for times of anxiety out in public. Since you can't always look at your bathroom mirror throughout the day, I encourage you to write down affirmations backing them up through God's word. You can write them down in your notes app on your phone or on a physical piece of paper and keep it in your purse or your pocket to always take with you. Read them whenever you are feeling anxious.

Writing down these verses and looking at them will eventually lead to memorization and having them in your head to dispute the lies Satan is whispering to you which is making you anxious and weighing you down. It is important to stay in the word for it is good and will calm your heart, giving you peace and creating happiness.

What is making you anxious today? Whatever it is, look up some verses to dispute those thoughts. Write them down so you have them readily accessible wherever you go. They might come in handy while dealing with life's challenges.

119

OPEN AND CLOSED DOORS

"I know your works. Behold, I have set before you an open door,
which no one is able to shut. I know that you have but little power,
and yet you have kept my word and have not denied my name."
Revelation 3:8

Have you ever heard the expression, "when one door closes, another one opens?" Well, it is true that sometimes God needs to close certain doors in our life to lead us to that open door down the hallway. And when it's the right door, according to God's will, there's no shutting it. On the other hand, when that door is shut, it is important to leave it closed and not try to force it open! Our job is to keep on searching for the door that God intends for us to travel through.

I think of this often with relationships. If God has made it clear that someone is not "the one," don't go back to them! I know it can be hard sometimes to start getting to know someone again. Trust me, that is me right now. I know there may be times where you want to go back to your ex because you know that is what is comfortable and familiar, but you must believe God shut that door for a reason. It is so important to honor that and trust that God knows better.

It's hard during a breakup because it's like the person was two different people. Or at least for me it was. There are the sweet memories that may make you miss him, but there's also the bad memories where you were crying day after day and stressed out of your mind. In times where I miss him, I remind myself of the place I was in when I was with him. I truly believe that God permitted my skin to break out so terribly to show me that this was not just affecting me mentally, but the continual stress was also affecting me physically. I remind myself that I owe it to myself to never go back to that state. That door is shut! When you find the right person, you will know it as you should feel a peace and certain tranquility that only

God can provide. You should not have to force it but when it's God's will, there's no stopping it.

Additionally, open and closed doors can also relate to your career. Something I've been doing along with acting and modeling is social media marketing. In addition to maintaining my own social media accounts, I have been working for several companies running their accounts and creating marketing reels to post for them. However, one of the biggest challenges is figuring out the algorithms to help increase visibility and marketability.

I am somewhat embarrassed to say that I take hundreds of pictures just to find "the one" that I actually post. That goes to show how social media is really people showing you what they want you to see. Sometimes even before posting, I'll ask some of my friends which of the last few that I'm deciding between are their favorite. However, in life, we really don't need the approval of others. Our confidence should only come from God. Don't seek your value from others. Instead, we should know that we are already approved by God.

I realize that sometimes I will nitpick too much by overthinking when I focus on a picture. When I finally post, I then start to pay attention to the "likes." Even if I personally loved the picture I posted, and I didn't get as many likes, it makes me think differently about the picture I just posted. We often forget that the algorithm changes. Years ago, I posted pictures and got way more likes than I do now, and yet I'm putting out better content now. Remember that the number of likes received is one person per like! Imagine that there are that many people coming up to you and complimenting you! I think we get so caught up in the number that we forget about the actual attention. I encourage you to put the "likes" mentality aside. Instead, focus on posting things that bring you happiness. I have always loved to post aesthetically pleasing things that make me smile. Social media can be a wonderful opportunity to make someone's day a little brighter, even yours. Just have fun with it! Try to drop all the unneeded pressure.

The hard part is yes, there is a little bit of pressure to have followers and likes if you're wanting to build a career out of it, but I think you need to trust that God will either bless it or He won't, and you should just enjoy it in the meantime.

If you are currently in a relationship where you find yourself debating if they're the one or not, I want you to pray this prayer. "Dear Lord, I pray that if this person is not meant to be my future partner, then I ask you to please remove them from my life." As hard as that prayer is to pray, it's better for God to remove them now rather than wasting your time. You will then be free to meet the person God truly has for you sooner than later. With my first boyfriend, I actually prayed this prayer, and he broke up with me the next day! It was hard for a minute, but I got over it. I'm not even kidding. A minute. I cried and then went to class. When you truly believe God will bless what is for you and remove what isn't, it's easier to move on.

Maybe you're single and not even thinking about a relationship right now and just focusing on your career. Pray that God opens the right doors for you and closes the wrong ones. I'm sure you've heard the saying "it's not rejection, it's redirection or God's protection." Now, when things don't go my way, I try my best not to be upset anymore because I know it wasn't mine to begin with and God has something better planned for me!

120

ENCOURAGEMENT THROUGH PRAYER

*"Therefore encourage one another and build one
another up, just as you are doing."*
1 Thessalonians 5:11

After reading today's verse, I realize there are multiple ways of encouraging someone. It can be as simple as giving someone a compliment or supporting them through prayer. Matthew 18:20 tells us that when two or more are gathered in My name, there am I among them. There is truly power in prayer.

Pastor Noah recently told a story about how someone came to his youth group wearing a boot due to having a sprained foot. During the service, they took prayer requests and all prayed over those who were ill and hurting, including the person with the injured foot. By the end of the service, that person felt healed, took off the boot, and started running around! God can and does perform miracles. There is power not only in numbers, but in directed prayer.

Another instance that brings tears to my eyes is at the end of 2023, world renowned dancer Derek Hough was on tour and during one of the numbers, a crew member came out to tell him that his wife, Hayley, wouldn't be coming on stage for the next number. Hayley was on the ground having seizures! She was rushed to the hospital, still in costume. It turned out that she had a brain bleed. It didn't look promising for his bride of just a few months. Thankfully she ended up having a successful surgery, but even so, the doctors said she may not ever walk again. Fans all over the world held her up in prayer. Hayley, being the "stubborn person" she calls herself, not only learned to walk again, but she was back to dancing on tour within only a few short months! I was fortunate to attend their postponed December tour this past May. Watching Hayley dance and knowing what she had endured was beyond moving. Their love story was also beautiful to capture as they were given the gift of being able to dance together once again. Those doctors told

Derek that his wife is truly a walking, or rather, a "dancing" miracle! Derek and Hayley continue to dance together and are stronger than ever! They were also certain to thank all their fans for praying. We are comforted to know that God hears our prayers, there is power in numbers, and of course, God will answer when we call upon Him.

How can you encourage someone today?

121

DAUGHTER OF THE KING

"All glorious is the princess in her chamber, with robes interwoven with gold. In many-colored robes she is led to the king."
Psalm 45:13

Growing up, I was always told that I was "Daddy's little princess," but the truth is, the only true King is God. Not your dad, not your boyfriend, or even a husband. Only God.

When I was young, I always loved princess movies and had tons of dress up clothes, always wearing gowns and tiaras along with pretty jewelry, purses, and heels. It's funny how now, not much has changed as I often model wedding dresses. If five-year-old Faith only knew that was going to be in her future, she would be elated and overjoyed.

Fun fact, these bridal photo shoots were done shortly after my breakup with my last boyfriend. Talk about the definition of Taylor Swift's lyrics, "I can do it with a broken heart." While it can be discouraging that I'm not getting married anytime soon like I had thought, it was a great confidence boost for me. Who doesn't want to put on a gorgeous gown? Plus, I now have an idea of what I want for whenever that day comes.

Also, here is a little tip, whether you have a guy in the picture now or not, it's never too soon to start working on your "wedding body." While I know all bodies are beautiful and anybody can be a "wedding body," I also know many people like to get in shape the year before their wedding. Just putting it out there that you won't have to do that if, instead, you are consistent with your diet and workouts now, perhaps years before the big day.

While the fancy gowns and appearance of a princess can seem magical, it is always said in the movies that it's not the crown that makes someone a princess, it's the heart and character that matters.

I've also always loved the expression, "Chin up, so your crown doesn't fall." I remember when I was struggling with my hormonal acne, I would sometimes walk with my head down as opposed to normally lifted and exuding confidence. This was very different for me, especially as a dancer. I would often receive compliments on my "walk" as I would always have my chin held high while walking with a purpose radiating confidence. As a daughter of the King, your confidence comes from the Lord! So, chin up, no matter what insecurities you may be facing.

Check your heart today. Are you portraying yourself as a daughter of the King? Are you showing yourself to be a good example of how Christians should act? Check your confidence. Are you letting your insecurities get the best of you or are you exuding confidence as a daughter of the King?

122

STRAIGHT TEETH, STRAIGHT PATHS

*"In all your ways acknowledge Him
and He will make straight your paths."*
Proverbs 3:6

Growing up, I got braces when I was 8 years old. They were only on the top four and bottom four teeth. As I got older and lost the rest, I was gifted a second set of braces on all my teeth, and they were removed at the end of junior high. I was lucky I had them young enough before I could really be insecure about myself. However, I know in many cases, people will stop smiling because they are insecure of their braces. Record numbers of people got braces during COVID as they were able to fix their teeth in private.

You deserve to smile! And for encouragement, keep in mind that it's only temporary. Be patient. And, be grateful. Your parents are most likely paying for them, and braces are not cheap. You're going to have stunning teeth coming out of this. It will be worth it!

It's interesting how some people need braces, and some do not. Regardless, we all need Jesus. Just like how braces will align our teeth, reading God's word and spending time with Him can lead to making our paths straight in life as well. But it takes time. There's a reason you don't have braces on for just a few days. They are needed for months, if not years, to move your teeth making them straight. Don't just show up to church on a Sunday expecting God to move things in your life. Spend consistent time with Him each day, even if it's just for a few minutes to begin. A habit to read and learn more will be formed, and your desire will be reinforced..

I encourage you to start by setting a timer for a minimum of 5 minutes each day this week, spending intentional time in His word. As you devote this time, my hope is the time increases each day.

PUSH YOURSELF

"But they who wait for the Lord shall renew their strength;
they shall mount up with wings like eagles; they shall run
and not be weary; they shall walk and not faint."
Isaiah 40:31

I have mentioned in previous devotions the importance of rest, especially when you are sick or injured. It's great to be disciplined in regard to going to the gym, but there are times where you need to listen to your body, let yourself heal or get better, and not push yourself.

If you're healthy, it is okay to go push yourself and workout! You will always feel better after exercising. You may regret not going to the gym, but no one ever says they regret that they went. It does so much for your physical health, but it is also great for your mental wellbeing, providing much-needed endorphins!

In today's culture of comparison via social media, it can be easy to get caught up in working out for the aesthetics verses working out to feel healthy leading to a better life. I encourage you to do it because God gave you the ability to workout. There's someone out there right now who wishes they could do what you can do. And if you ever "don't feel like it," remember today's verse that "they shall run and not be weary." Ask God for the energy, strength, and stamina to push through your workouts and you will not only feel better, but you are honoring the Lord and you won't regret it!

Before your workout today, pray to God thanking Him for your healthy body that allows you to push yourself.

124

SLOW TO SPEAK

*"Know this, my beloved brothers: let every person be quick
to hear, slow to speak, slow to anger; for the anger of
man does not produce the righteousness of God."*
James 1:19

Sometimes, we are so quick to speak that we forget to listen to what someone has to say. Even when it comes to God, it is one thing to pray and bring forth your requests to God, but are you willing to sit still in the silence of listening to what He may be saying to you? Some may ask, how do you hear God? Well, this often occurs through the Holy Spirit who may orchestrate thoughts that pop into your mind. We need to practice being better listeners than speakers, especially when it comes to not knowing others' stories.

One of my favorite actresses from the Disney Channel when I was little was Selena Gomez. In addition to being an actress and a singer, she now has 423 million Instagram followers, founder of Rare Beauty, and the CIO/founder of Wondermind focusing on mental health on Instagram. Selena's Instagram bio states, "By grace, through faith."

When someone has this many followers, you are bound to have some negative comments. Coming from my generation especially, we watched her play a fifteen-year-old on Disney Channel and of course she looks different now than she did many years ago. Selena has been very open about her diagnosis of having lupus. She shares about the medication she takes which causes her to have water retention out of her control. She has also shared about having Small Intestinal Bacterial Overgrowth (SIBO) which also flares up. I have even seen people in several recent videos of her where they speculate that she's pregnant. Clearly it is just a bad angle, or what she was wearing, or she was a little bloated from the water weight caused by her meds. What I love about Selena is that she's real and transparent with all her followers. She is just like everyone else and has her own hurdles. It is important not to be so quick to judge because you truly never know what someone is going through.

Today, when someone is talking to you, I want you to actively listen to what they are saying and be slow to speak. Maybe you have a friend or family member going through a hardship. You don't always have to be a "fixer." Sometimes, they just need someone to listen.

FOR HIS GLORY

"As each has received a gift, use it to serve one another,
as good stewards of God's varied grace."
1 Peter 4:10

A few devotions back, I discussed how God has given each person a gift. These can be seen as talents, skills, unique capabilities, etc. So, here's the question…how are you using your gift? Are you using it for your own pleasures and benefits, or are you using it to serve others and bring honor and glory to Christ?

I thought it was only fitting to have this devotion be based on Justin Bieber as I had mentioned his former girlfriend, Selena Gomez, earlier. I love how Justin has truly changed for the better. Justin knows that he is not defined by his past and that we have a merciful God who forgives us and loves us before we did anything to even deserve it. I love how he talks about this "free gift" and the message of the gospel even during his concerts where he has also added more worship music to his set lists.

Justin has always had the gift of singing, but to see him use it to bring people to Christ is how God truly wants to see us use our gifts. I think it's so amazing, especially for those who knew Justin before he started talking about God and his faith. Those who were non-believers and are still following him are having the opportunity to hear the message of the gospel and see how God has changed his life and then contemplate how God can easily change theirs as well.

How can you use your gift to not only bring glory to the Lord, but to serve others? Maybe you're not a singer, but you have the gift of writing or speaking. You can share your testimony with others. Let others know how God changed your life, giving you hope as He helped you through the hardships.

126

PUT ON CHRIST

"But put on the Lord Jesus Christ, and make no
provision for the flesh, to gratify its desires."
Romans 13:14

I'm sure you have heard the expression before, "Be true to who you are." In fact, when I was in 8th grade, I performed a dance to that song. I do think it is a great message, especially focusing on middle schoolers who are teens in a developmental stage trying to find out who they are.

Sometimes, we pretend to be like someone we're not just for the sake of fitting in. It's easy to look the part. Take Halloween for example, whether that be putting on a costume, playing dress-up, or wearing a mask to a masquerade party. Ask the question, "Who am I, deep down?"

Maybe it's not a physical mask or one's appearance in general. Perhaps you know someone who is pretending to be someone they're not through their character. In Matthew 7:15, we are warned to "Beware of false prophets, who come to you in sheep's clothing but inwardly are ravenous wolves."

It's a shame how many people on social media can "put on a mask" acting fake, just to get followers or likes. Or even in person, people may pretend to be nice to you only to get something out of you. I always try my best to be authentic and genuine, and if anyone ever thinks I'm fake, they clearly don't know me. Generally, I typically have a bubbly personality. The only time I may "paste on a smile" is if I'm having a rough day yet still want to bring joy to others not bringing attention to my struggle.

Nowhere in the Bible did Jesus say to be "true to who you are." This statement is actually false as we should never be true to our fallen selves, rather we need to be true to His word in which the Bible tells us to live our lives.

The best thing to put on is not the new trendy clothes, the costume, the dress-up, the mask, etc., but rather "put on the Lord Jesus Christ," as today's verse instructs us to do. Forget wanting to be like someone else, we should spend each day making a conscious effort to live our lives as Christ would. Let's all be more like Jesus!

How can you display Christ through your actions today?

127

I JUST WANT JESUS TO COME BACK

"But you are not in darkness, brothers, for that
day to surprise you like a thief."
1 Thessalonians 5:4

Have you ever heard an elderly person say to you, "I am so glad I didn't grow up in a world like this?" Coming from someone who is younger and is growing up in today's world, it's like, what am I supposed to say to that? Well, that's good for you! I do, however, must grow up in today's world where everything seems much more expensive than when you grew up. Not to mention, everything is far more complex.

Or maybe you've heard someone say, "we are definitely approaching the end times!" Some believe in "Murphy's Law" where anything that can go wrong will go wrong. Having this negative mindset like "our world is hopeless," is only feeding that idea. Instead, we should get our hopes up that things can get better, and God is in control. We can't have faith, if we don't also have hope.

When I was dealing with my hormonal acne, I was in a very bad mental state not only dealing with my insecurity, but also during a roller coaster relationship, trying to figure out my career, and just putting unneeded pressure on myself. I often said during these times, "I just want Jesus to come back." As the world is continuing to face more and more hardship, you may hear others also say similar phrases, which is sort of an "I give up" mindset.

The thing is, this is an extremely selfish mindset to have as we are called to spread the gospel and lead others to know Christ and join us in heaven one day as well. During these hard times, people need encouragement, and this good news of the gospel can change their lives and where they spend their eternity. Jesus will come back once everyone has had a chance to hear the gospel, and with social media, we are able to reach more people now than ever before and its only going to continue. As it says on today's verse, Jesus will come back "like a thief." Some translations say, "as a thief in the night." The point is, we don't know when He is coming back, so we need to be ready!

And as you are waiting in this world full of sin and hardship, where it can be easy to just want to go to heaven now or have Christ come back, have a hopeful mindset that things on earth can get better as we have faith in Him.

Next time you are thinking, "I wish Jesus would just come back already," switch your mindset to "who have I not told about Jesus Christ yet who needs saving?" Share the gospel with that person and pray for that person's salvation as there is power in prayer and I have seen people do complete 180's and become a Christian after lots of consistent prayer.

128

BOLD FAITH

*"In whom we have boldness and access with
confidence through our faith in Him."*
Ephesians 3:12

In a previous devotion, I spoke briefly about my parents choosing my name "Faith" and how they prayed the verse Hebrews 11:1, *"Now faith is the assurance of things hoped for, the conviction of things not seen."* While my mom was trying to get pregnant, she had originally chosen my name to be Hannah because Hannah was barren in the bible. Before my mom was pregnant, her friend had a baby and took the name. My mom said she was sad, but she knew that she couldn't claim a name when she wasn't pregnant. A few years later, that same friend had a second baby and named her Grace. What was ironic was the fact that Grace was the new name my mom had chosen should she get pregnant and have a baby girl. But again, she wasn't angry, she was just a little sad. My mom saw so many of her friends having babies, and I heard her once say she attended 27 baby showers. The fact that she knew that number shows what a painful "waiting" season it was for her.

For nine years, she was patient, she prayed, and she waited on the Lord. She even prayed to the Lord to take the desire away from her if she wasn't going to be blessed with a child. God had different plans as she finally became pregnant and then I was born on March 19th, 2002. She named me "Faith" as she had bold faith knowing that at the right time, God would bless her with a baby. I couldn't have asked for a better name as it is so intentional. Additionally, my last name is Bolde, pronounced Bold-ie, however it is often mispronounced as Bold. So, my name really is "Bold(e), Faith." I have always joked that I will only marry someone with a last name that starts with a "B" as I want to keep my initials "FAB." My parents didn't even put it together that my last name could be Bold, and it wasn't until they dedicated me at church when the pastor asked what my middle name was and when they said

Abigail, the pastor declared, "I love it! FAB! (Like Fabulous.)" As a kid, one of my favorite movies was *High School Musical,* and I was totally a little Sharpay. For anyone who has seen the movie, you are probably familiar with the song that Sharpay sings, "Fabulous." I would always sing around the house while dressed in an all-pink outfit or having friends over making them be the other characters while I was always the main character, Sharpay.

I am so grateful for my name as it is a constant reminder to be bold in my faith no matter what hardship I am facing. I am also reminded that my mom had to wait patiently for me, just like I had to wait for clear skin. God will give you what is in His will in His perfect timing. The hard part is being patient in the meantime.

Are you bold in your faith? Does your name mean something to you? Do you realize that calling yourself a Christian is how you are defined just like your reputation reflects your last name as it represents your family?

BEAUTY AND BRAINS

"Now the name of the man was Nabal, and the name of his
wife Abigail. The woman was discerning and beautiful, but the
man was harsh and badly behaved; he was a Calebite."
1 Samuel 25:3

My mom got my middle name from the woman Abigail in the Bible, described as not only beautiful, but intelligent. I have spoken in a past devotion about my insecurity of how some of my friends would roast me in high school for saying something perhaps a little ditsy and assuming I was not smart. It didn't help when many of their mothers would also play into it adding, "it's a good thing you're pretty." Whether someone says it as a joke or not, there is always a little bit of truth behind it and that carried with me throughout my education, often causing me to doubt myself thinking I'll never be as smart as the others.

Fast forward a few years later, I graduated Magna Cum Laude with a bachelor's degree in film production with a concentration in screenwriting from California Baptist University. This proved to me that I can do hard things, and I am more than "just a pretty face." I am so grateful to my parents for giving me such an intentional name with not just Bold Faith, but also the middle name Abigail, reminding me that I am both beautiful and smart.

Maybe today you feel like you're beautiful, but not smart enough. Or maybe you feel the opposite and think you're smart but not pretty. I am telling you today that you are both! You are a beautiful creation in God's eyes, and He has blessed you not just with beauty, but a brain!

130

CHRISTIAN

*"Yet if anyone suffers as a Christian, let him not be
ashamed, but let him glorify God in that name."*
1 Peter 4:16

As we have just talked about names the past few days, I want to end this series
with reminding you of the best name of all, Christian. Now, if your name is
actually Christian, props to you, but that doesn't make you a Christ-follower.
To become a Christian, we must believe in the gospel of Jesus Christ that He
died on the cross for our sins, and three days later He rose again, so that if we
believe in Him, we too may live in heaven one day.

When we call ourselves a Christian, we should take pride in that name as
a Christ-follower. Oftentimes, part of being a Christian means going through
hardships as the enemy tries to attack us. However, this only grows our faith
and our trust in God. Do not be ashamed when you suffer as a Christian,
but rather find encouragement knowing whom your faith is in, and that He
will help you through it, turning your hardships for your good, and for His
glory through your testimony.

It's not always "sunshine and rainbows" being a Christian. In fact,
sometimes it may look like the direct opposite of that. However, we know
we can lean on God during the storm, and that at the end of all of this, our
eternity lies in heaven with Him.

*Can you call yourself a Christian? If not, let today be the day that you
accept Christ into your life. We are never promised tomorrow or even the
next moment for that matter, and we don't know when Jesus is coming
back. Don't let it be too late. Accept Christ as your Lord and Savior
right now.*

CONFIDENCE

*"For the Lord will be your confidence and will
keep your foot from being caught."*
Proverbs 3:26

Have you ever heard the expression, "Walk into the room like God sent you?" That's the level of confidence you should have. However, I was listening to a Sadie Robertson podcast recently and she said something that really spoke to me. She said that we should be a "there she is person" instead of a "here I am" person. Her reasoning was meant to say that we can still be humble while also being confident.

Maybe you've heard another common expression, "Look in the mirror, that's your competition." Sadie also talked about in her podcast how you should stop looking over your shoulder or to your left or to your right because you are an original! It is so important to not compare yourself to others. God made you exactly the way you are supposed to be.

In this particular podcast episode, she had Reece Weaver from the Dallas Cowboys Cheerleaders as her guest, whom I have talked about in a past devotional. Reece talks about how she grew up watching the show *Dallas Cowboys Cheerleaders Making the Team* and the first time she went to AT&T stadium and saw the field, she turned to her mom and said, "I'm gonna be down there one day."

Talk about confidence! Reece explains the tryout process as she just gave it to God whether He would open that door for her or not. Having moved past the first round of virtual auditions, she thought, well this isn't a no, maybe this is possible. As she approached the second round of virtual auditions, her prayer was to just make it to the in-person auditions. Even if she experienced rejection, at least she knew she could get there. From making it to the in-person auditions to training camp, she talks about how it is very real to have a little bit of nerves and anxiety. At these times, you need to ignore the lies the enemy is telling you, trying to make you doubt yourself or compare yourself to the other dancers you're up against, and just focus on yourself and remain confident. Be confident in the fact that if it is God's will, He will make it happen. She just wanted God to use her and for Him to be glorified through it all.

In a separate podcast, I heard an Olympic athlete talk about how the feeling we get when we're nervous is the exact feeling we get when we're excited and have adrenaline. The only difference is our mindset. So, if you can change your mindset from being nervous, to using that adrenaline and being excited, you'll perform better and be more confident. I wish I had heard that back in my dance competition days because I got insanely stressed right before I was set to perform.

I was recently asked what my favorite year was when I was dancing and, ironically, I think it was before eighth grade when I was just doing studio dance. As awesome as it is to call myself a seven-year National Champion, three of those years being a Division 1 collegiate athlete, also came with a lot of pressure. Some parents may be the ones putting that pressure on their kids, but for me, it was self-inflicted as I have always been hard on myself. It's ironic that I ended my dance career, and I say this with humility, at a level of being at the best I had ever been in my dance career, yet I enjoyed it the least. It's a shame to see so many athletes burn out because of the pressure they put on themselves, or maybe it's not even about the sport and it's about the drama within the sport. I still have a great love for dance, and I know that I always will.

Like Reece, something that always got me through competitions was having the mindset to do the best I can to honor the Lord through my gift and leave the placement up to the judges. I was also very blessed that many of my dance teachers and coaches, especially in college, were Christians themselves and would pray before our performances. Reece describes the Dallas Cowboy Cheerleaders as a "sisterhood," so much so that some of them have Bible studies together. I really do think there is something so special about dancing with other "sisters in Christ," a group of girls who can uplift you and, in return, it allows you to dance more confidently as well.

What are you competing for right now? Whether that be your sport, applications to colleges, job interviews, whatever it may be, be confident in knowing that if it is God's will, He will make it happen, and let Him use you, and let Him be glorified through it all. Just do your best and give it all to Him.

132

PICK ME

"It is not good to eat much honey, nor is it glorious to seek one's own glory."
Proverbs 25:27

Continuing to talk about confidence, one of the least attractive things one can do is be a "pick me" person, also known as one who is often "fishing for compliments." For instance, if someone says, "Ugh, my hair turned out so bad today," they are waiting for their friend listening to them to say, "No, it looks good," giving them the reassurance they were looking for.

When I was struggling with my hormonal acne, I heard girls complain about their skin. It bothered me so much as I knew full well that they were only overreacting about one blemish opposed to my struggle with my entire lower face breaking out.

Even if you are insecure about something, the most confident thing you can do is to own it. Most people are so self-absorbed that others probably would not even notice. Be confident in yourself. It even says in today's verse that we shouldn't be seeking our own glory through other people's validation. We only need affirmation from the Lord.

It can be easy to want to be "people pleasers" having everyone like us whether that be based on our actions or on our appearances. Believe me, I know that all too well. I would consider myself a likeable person, so in the rare chance someone doesn't particularly like me, I am very confused and hurt. In moments like these, just remember that more than likely they have their own problems, and you are not necessarily the issue. It is hard to accept but show kindness anyway and remember that you are special, uniquely designed, and crafted by the Creator.

Check in with yourself today. Are you seeking validation from others, or from God?

NAVIGATION

"The steps of a man are established by the
Lord, when he delights in his way."
Psalm 37:23

One day, I was driving to a friend's house, and it was raining. I had the navigation set on my phone, and I was aware that sometimes when it is raining, accidents are more common. I knew that there was a significant chance that I could be rerouted. As I got closer to the house, it said I was only three miles away, yet it would take thirty minutes to get there. I was very confused. I didn't realize it at the time, but my car's Global Positioning System (GPS) was taking me to the back of the house (which was a very rural road), instead of the front of the house on the actual streets. I trusted the GPS so much that I ended up on a one-way dirt fire road on the side of a steep hill, getting my car stuck in mud from the pouring rain. To make matters worse, nobody was around to help me. Additionally, there wasn't the best cell service for getting texts through. Praise the Lord as a phone call finally went through to get AAA to come save me. By far, one of the least intelligent things I have ever done.

Sometimes, we rely too heavily on our GPS. We take for granted that our satellite reception is always going to be there. We often count on things that are not dependable. The only one we can always depend on is God. In life, God doesn't always show us our destination because He wants us to depend on Him. Let God guide your steps and be your navigator. For me, I have really had to rely on God in many situations. And you know what? He always comes through. Sometimes, He asks us to be patient and that is always very hard. I know that when I was struggling with my hormonal acne, I had to rely on Him a lot. I didn't know when my skin would be clear again, but I trusted He knew that this really affected me, and it was something that I needed to place in His trust. I prayed for God to guide my next steps whether it be using certain skincare, supplements, medication, etc. Obviously, He didn't say, "Faith you need to take medication now." However, He led me down several roads where I needed to research and learn as much as I could on my own because He was the one who gave me a brain. I never really liked science in school, but I have been struck by how much I enjoy learning about how things affect my body whether it be certain foods, weather, and even stress. One thing that I embrace now more than anything is knowing that the Lord is the ultimate GPS... God Positioning System.

What "destination" are you worried about getting to that you need to surrender to God? Are you believing He will get you there and praying that He will guide your next steps in the meantime?

134

FIVE HITS A DAY

"Whatever you do, work heartily, as for the Lord and not for men."
Colossians 3:23

When we wake up every day, it is a gift from God. It's a blessing and an opportunity just waiting for us to claim. However, how you choose to use your time during the day will determine your ultimate outcome. You see, we are called as Christ-followers to be good stewards of the time that God affords us each day. We should be striving to bring glory to the Lord as we use our time, talents, and treasures. I recently listened to a podcast of Christian speaker Terri Savelle Foy, talking about her morning routine. She used the example that if you were to go out with an axe and swing five times at a tree each day, it might not fall on the first day, but it will eventually over time.

The rule about either starting or breaking habits is that you must be consistent with it for at least 21 days. One habit that Terri talked about is how she listened to a faith building message every day for 21 days, which then turned into 30 days, and then two months, and then three months. That was back in 2002, and she hasn't stopped since. In one of those messages she listened to, she heard a statement made by John Maxwell that changed her life forever. He said, "If I could come to your house and just watch you for 24 hours, I could tell whether or not you're going to be a success or a failure." What do your daily habits look like?

The second habit Terri talks about is reading. I relate to Terri in a way where she never loved to read for pleasure. So, she set the timer on her phone for 20 minutes and made herself sit down and read. The first few days were torture for her, but after a while she realized the more she read, the more she learned, and the more she learned, the more she began to earn. Over the next 11 years of her life, her income more than quadrupled, she got a massive promotion, she went from ghost writing books for her dad to authoring books. She went from attending conferences to speaking at conferences and went from watching TV for hours to being on a television show. As she began to grow, everything else in her life began to grow as well. It is so important to keep educating yourself.

The third habit Terri talked about was exercise! She says that it is more than just the physical aspect, it is also great for "building your self-esteem, reducing stress, improving your sleep, boosting your memory and concentration, and simply making you happier." One thing that I loved was when she said, "Stop looking at the one hour you don't have, look at the 20 minutes you do have and get moving!" I relate to this in the sense that I am such a routine based person where I work out an hour and a half to two hours every day, and if my schedule doesn't allow for that entire workout, I get mad at myself. But the truth is, something is better than nothing. Just move your body every day in some way, even if it's just for a few minutes. You don't have to do the same two hours every day. Some days may be shorter. Just keep showing up for yourself and have that dedication and consistency.

The fourth habit Terri talked about was praying and meditating. We've talked about this in a previous devotion where it is easy to pray and talk to God, but meditating is listening to God. One way to do this is to journal about everything that God places on your mind.

And finally, the fifth habit Terri talked about was writing down your dreams and goals. Tony Robbins says that "setting goals is the first step at turning the invisible into the visible." Terri says that physically writing down your goals on paper "forces you to get specific about your ambitions."

Doing these five habits every day, will make you successful, just like hitting that tree five times a day will make it eventually come toppling down. I've seen many similar challenges before like the "75 hard" started by Andy Frisella, where you follow a diet, do two workouts a day (one being outside), take progress pictures, drink a gallon of water a day, and read 10 pages of a book each day. Whatever challenge or daily habits you implement into your life, let it all be for God's glory as you seek Him in all that you do.

Write down each of your daily habits that you implement in your everyday life.

135

ASK FOR FORGIVENESS

"Bearing with one another and, if one has a complaint against another, forgiving each other; as the Lord has forgiven you, so you also must forgive."
Colossians 3:13

I feel like a lot of dancers can relate to this when I say I am guilty of acting like a brat on dance competition days, especially to my mom. This didn't even start happening until I started high school. I know that it's because of the pressure I would put on myself. I'm sure you've heard the expression "bride-zilla," toward brides on their wedding days or just referencing people who lash out when they're stressed. It is during these times that we must ask for forgiveness.

Even though I'm not in the dance world anymore, I'm now in the film industry, which can also be stressful at times. Especially coming from someone who likes a schedule, it can be tough for me with last minute schedule modifications or time changes, early call times or late nights, and a multitude of other "inconveniences." It isn't like a 9-5 job where you can have your routine and same schedule every day.

As we discussed in the last devotion about daily habits, I am a very routine based person who has an internal checklist of things I do daily. On a day being on set (so thankful it's not every day), I would get stressed about maybe not getting my full eight hours of sleep the night before since sometimes the call times would be late or last minute, and then the call times would generally be early. I would also get stressed about perhaps missing a workout as days on set can be very long. I would also get stressed about the food and whether it was something I could eat. As a result, I generally would bring my own snacks.

The point is, knowing I have a stressful day ahead, I could sometimes inadvertently lash out toward others or my poor mom the night before. When this happens, I always feel bad and apologize right away asking for forgiveness. I am grateful that she forgives me, just as God has forgiven us. My mom is a counselor, and she can easily recognize that yes, although it is nice to have daily habits to "check off" every day, it isn't always realistic. I know that I need to learn to be more adaptable and that I'm almost superstitious where I tend to believe that if I don't do them, something bad will happen. Truly it is controlling what can be controlled, and sometimes that can turn into OCD which I am working on. I must pray to God to help me in this area because I do become so routine oriented that I am often quick to fly off the handle when it is really the most minute of things that I am upset about. I need to look more at the big picture when these things catch me off guard.

Have you ever taken your anger out on someone who didn't deserve it, just because you were under pressure or in a stressful situation? Reflect on whether you took the time to ask for forgiveness. If you hadn't, ask the person you wronged for forgiveness. Then, take the time to thank God for His forgiveness toward you too.

136
BEAUTY STANDARDS

"Because you are precious in my eyes,
and honored, and I love you."
Isaiah 43:4

Someone who brings up a lot of mixed opinions generating much controversy is Taylor Swift. People seem to love her or hate her. Especially among Christ-followers. Many stopped listening to her music as they thought it was dishonoring the Lord. In the Bible, we are told to be cautious of what we consume whether it be what we are watching or what we are listening to. I think Taylor Swift has some good songs, so where do you draw the line of which songs of hers you should or shouldn't listen to? I listen to the Holy Spirit inside of me and if a song convicts me, feeling like I shouldn't be listening to it, I turn it off and I choose not to listen to it.

Love her or hate her, I really respect her intellect. Clearly, she is incredibly smart as she methodically plans out so many things. She is extremely intentional when it comes to the smallest details… of her music, her tour plans, and how she builds relationships with her team. As Christians, we are also called to love all. That doesn't mean we need to agree with others' political beliefs. We also need to realize and remember that everyone makes mistakes. We certainly should never show hate. Unfortunately, when one is in the spotlight, hate often accompanies it.

Taylor spoke out about her previous eating disorder, back in her documentary *Miss Americana*, released in 2020. She states, "There's always some standard of beauty that you're not meeting. Cause if you're thin enough, then you don't have that (booty) that everybody wants, but if you have enough weight on you to have a (booty), then your stomach isn't flat enough. It's all just…impossible." People would comment that she was too thin, but now that she has gained healthy weight, some will point out that she's gained weight. The best thing you can do is just ignore the comments, ignore the beauty standards, and be grateful for what God has given you, for in His eyes, we are preciously made, and He loves us just the way we are.

Do a quick audit of what you are listening to and watching. Think about editing some of your choices if you feel the Holy Spirit convicting you. A few things I always ask myself are, "Does this glorify God?" and "Does this show myself as a good role model to others?"

137

GRATEFUL

"I give you thanks, O Lord, with my whole heart;
before the gods I sing your praise."
Psalm 138:1

As we enter the last week of this devotional, I want to reflect on how far I have come since the beginning of writing these entries. That girl back then was heartbroken. She was struggling with the insecurity of her skin breaking out. She was crying nearly every day. Months later, I am in a much better place. My relationship with God has grown so much. Yes, my skin has been getting clearer, but I have learned that when I relied on God, He gave me hope. He is in control of everything. I can't even remember the last time I cried. If you had told me a few months ago when my skin was at its worst that I would be in a new relationship and my acne wouldn't consume my day, I wouldn't have believed you. This just goes to show that things can and will get better! God is in the details, and He alone gives us hope.

Anyone who has had severe acne before knows that it can be a traumatic experience. Oftentimes, it is natural to self-sabotage yourself, fearing that it may come back. In times like these, be grateful in the present moment. I like to pray something like this, "Lord, thank you for getting me to where I am now. I don't know what the future may hold, but I know who holds my future."

One of my favorite worship songs that goes well with today's verse is "This Is How I Thank the Lord" by Mosaic MSC. The lyrics are, "This is how I thank the Lord for saving me, when I was weak, so I will sing." Whatever stage or season you may be in your life today, I encourage you to listen to this song and take a few moments thanking God for where you are right now taking solace in the fact that He cares for you and knows your future. What a relief to have that burden lifted.

138

GOD OF PEACE

"For God is not a God of confusion but of peace."
1 Corinthians 14:33

I had mentioned in a previous devotion how my motto has always been, "When you meet the right guy, you'll glow, but when it's the wrong guy, you'll get uglier." Not really, but in a previous relationship, I was constantly stressed. It is proven that stress is not good for the body and more than likely didn't help my acne. I knew that God was "not a God of confusion but of peace." Yet, at the same time, there were a lot of green flags accompanying the red flags which kept leading me to thinking that perhaps this was "the one" God had for me.

Little did I know that a few months later, I would find someone even better that God had for me. I have heard many times that God will always give you back better than what you have lost. I don't know of scripture that supports that, but I do know that God cares about every detail in my life and He will give me what He thinks is best for me. I know a lot of girls can be like this, not just me; but maturing truly is realizing that a guy who gives you peace and comfort where your body isn't in fight or flight 24/7 is much better than chasing a guy, even though "the chase" is often fun. Besides, the sooner you get rid of the wrong guy, the sooner you'll let God open that door for the right one.

They always say, you find that person when you are least expecting it. I wasn't even looking for a relationship, but when it's God's will, there's no stopping it. This is another reason why I love this devotional as it was originally just for me. However, as I wrote I realized that many girls would benefit from it if I were to publish it. I know that others are going through similar scenarios, and I just want to bring encouragement to them as well. It will be interesting to revisit these devotional journal entries in the future and to see if I am still with this same amazing guy and if he will be there in the end.

Regardless, I think each person God sends into our life is for a reason. I think you can learn from past relationships. It is important to figure out what you want in a relationship as much as it is important to know what you don't want in a future partner. In my current relationship, I am realizing what is important to me. I like the way he treats me. He makes me feel at peace. I believe that is one of the signs that this relationship is from God compared to others. My current relationship also reminds me of my worth. This man treats me the way I want to be treated, he wants to protect me, he wants to provide for me, and most importantly, he loves God even more than me. And let's not forget his southern charm! I've learned that you should never lower the bar. As a Chrisitan, my bar is set so high that I confidently know that God will give me exactly who he wants to be with me. Sometimes it is hard to get over past relationships. It is important to simply forgive previous relationships, move on, and run towards what God has for you!

No relationship is going to be perfect, even those social media couples or families you may see online. Instead of thinking of finding the right kind of person, think more about becoming and being the right kind of person. I always put so much pressure on myself to find "the one," but the truth is, I think there are many different possibilities of people who could be your potential partner. It is up to you to make it work, and the best way to make that happen is keeping Christ at the center of that relationship.

Whether it be a romantic relationship or just a friendship, evaluate the people around you and whether they bring you peace. God is not a God of chaos, find people who make you feel at ease. Trust me, your body, your skin, and nervous system will thank you too!

139

A MESS THAT'S BLESSED

"And to know the love of Christ that surpasses knowledge,
that you may be filled with all the fullness of God."
Ephesians 3:19

In a previous devotion, I wrote about Madison Prewett Trout who was on the 24th season of *The Bachelor* (Peter's season) which premiered in 2020. Well, it just so happens that Peter was one of the final three men of an earlier bachelorette, Hannah Brown, in 2019.

Besides being "The Bachelorette," Hannah Brown was also on Season 28 of *Dancing with The Stars* and ended up winning. She had also competed in many pageants having won the title of Miss Alabama in 2018. Since then, she has written a few books, including the one I recently read, *God Bless This Mess* (2021).

When people think of Hannah Brown as the Bachelorette, I would say one word to describe her is "iconic." This can be for multiple reasons, but one of my favorite moments was when she was called out by one of the men for something that she did and her response to him was, "...and Jesus still loves me." We are all imperfect human beings. We all make mistakes. And we should be very thankful that God shows us mercy and forgives us. I think it is so refreshing seeing someone claim their faith on national television, and then write a book about instances where her faith was tested on top of that!

In *God Bless This Mess*, Hannah is extremely vulnerable, talking about many hardships she had experienced throughout her life, beginning in childhood. I included a few other women, Demi Tebow and Lauren Norris, who were also in pageants. Now Hannah also speaks about her own anxiety and depression she faced during her years of pageantry.

In her chapter "Breakup Skinny," Hannah talks about losing a lot of weight after one of her breakups because she couldn't eat. To take her mind off things, her mom suggested that she'd do something fun like competing for the title of Miss Alabama again. This reminded me of the amazing opportunity afforded me in the world of wedding dress modeling right after one of my breakups. Generally, pageants take lots of preparation, and this pageant was only two weeks away. Hannah states, "I did love being onstage. I loved performing. Even though I had stopped doing pageants and slipped into a period of depression, in part because of the pressures of the pageant world, I remembered those few minutes onstage as being some of my happiest moments ever." I think of my dance competition days when despite the anxiety I would get, I still loved to perform.

Once she agreed to do the pageant, she and her mom pulled everything together, and when it was time for pageant day, lots of people there noticed she had lost a lot of weight, being at the lowest competition weight she's ever been at. She states that every person she ran into told her, "Wow, Hannah. You are stunning! How did you get so skinny?" She would tell them that it wasn't intentional, and it was due to her breakup, and they would immediately add, "Ohhhh… breakup skinny is the best kind of skinny. Good for you!" Personally, this is why I don't think comments should be made about anyone, especially regarding their appearance, because even if it is meant as a compliment, you never know what someone is really going through. Hannah said that she took their compliments in stride as she knew that they didn't know the details.

Hannah ended up winning the title of Miss Alabama at this particular pageant. Ironically, this time was when she and her mom threw it all together at the last minute. Hannah states that she felt less pressure at this pageant and just wanted to have fun. She says, "After the last few years of trying so hard to look and act like somebody else, I walked in as myself, and I won. I won by being me." This instance also reminded me of my dance competition days where sometimes I had so much anxiety and pressure leading up to the event that my body would physically shut down and I would get sick. I always became very nervous, especially whenever I had to perform my solo. During one competition I was running on Dayquil because I felt like I was coming down with something and was trying not to feel sick. Wouldn't you know, I ended up placing with my solo, doing the best I had ever done. Perhaps the medicine calmed my nerves? Ha, although I don't suggest that you try this if you aren't actually sick. But like Hannah, we both executed better when there was less pressure.

Looking at today's verse, may you be reminded that you are loved beyond measure by God, and just like Hannah Brown says, "Jesus still loves me," despite how much of a mess you may feel at times.

140
REMEMBER WHERE YOU STARTED

"Rejoice in hope, be patient in tribulation, be constant in prayer."
Romans 12:12

Back when I was struggling with my hormonal acne, there were lots of ups and downs. One minute I thought it was getting better, and the next, there was a new breakout. The esthetician I saw would take progress pictures each time I came in which helped a lot, reminding me of where I started and how far I've come. Sometimes, it can be hard to see the changes because it's not overnight, it's gradual.

Maybe for you it's not your skin but it's trying to lose weight or gain weight, maybe you're battling an illness, maybe you are trying to learn a new skill, or maybe you become overwhelmed by just reading a book. Whatever it may be, don't forget where you started and remember to celebrate the little victories toward your end goal. Have hope that God will get you there, be patient, and pray consistently. That being said, while placing your faith in God, still do what you can based on what God has given you, whether that be using your brain to research different skincare lines or supplements to achieve clear skin, or if it is choosing healthy food and working out for your fitness goals, or learning small bits of information at a time, listening to the doctors' orders for any illness, or reading a few pages of a book each day.

I encourage you to take progress pictures or journal for whatever gradual journey you are on. These will help you in times of discouragement to see how far you have come with the help of God, and a reminder that if He has gotten you that far, He can get you to the end.

141

STRONG AND COURAGEOUS

"Be strong and courageous. Do not fear or be in dread of them, for it is the Lord your God who goes with you. He will not leave you or forsake you."
Deuteronomy 31:6

As we reach the last few days of this devotional, here is a letter to someone going through a hardship. I wish I could have had this to help me through each day before I started writing this devotional.

Dear beautiful child of God, sitting on her bed right now, crying over her skin, relationship, and all the worries and stressors of life. Let God wipe your tears away, and lift your head, knowing you are a daughter of the King.

You were created in His image and are beautiful just as God intentionally took His time creating you. Even so, you are not defined by your external appearance, but by your heart and love for God.

He loves you so much and He will never leave you. Through all the trials that life has to offer, remember that God is with you, and you don't have to carry the worries.

I know looking at the uncertainty of the future can be frightening, but be strong and courageous, knowing that God already has everything taken care of according to His plan and His timing.

I encourage you to bookmark this page to come back to any time you need quick encouragement once you are done reading this devotional.

142

LEAN ON GOD

"God is our refuge and strength, a very present help in trouble."
Psalm 46:1

In the previous devotion, we discussed being strong and courageous during life's hardships. But where do we find our strength when we are weak? From the Lord. I remember one of the first songs I learned in Sunday school when I was little was "Jesus Loves Me," with the lyrics, "they are weak, but He is strong!" Worship music is often filled with scripture and this is why it's so important to also listen to worship music because the words will become ingrained in your memory throughout your entire life and will often come to mind when you need them the most as a reminder and encouragement.

When we come across a troubling situation and don't know what to do, ask God for His help. He is right there in your presence. He will get you through whatever you are going through. Lean on Him and let Him be your strength, fighting your battles for you. Let Him also be where you find peace and comfort, knowing that He has already taken care of whatever it is that's troubling you, and nothing is impossible with God.

Listen to "Jesus Loves Me" today by Chris Tomlin.

143

NOTHING'S IMPOSSIBLE WITH GOD

"For nothing will be impossible with God."
Luke 1:37

If there is one thing you got out of this devotional, I pray that you remember nothing is impossible with God. Back when I started this devotional, I thought I would never have clear skin again. Only God!

Just when you think something could never happen, think, "Only God!" Our God is a good God and sometimes He will have us experience harder seasons to grow, get closer to Him, or bring others to know Him. It is never without reason. Had I not struggled with my skin, I would have never written this devotional.

God's timing is truly everything and seeing where I was at when I started writing this devotional versus where I'm at now makes me feel extremely proud of myself and grateful to God.

I pray that this devotional did the same for you as well. Perhaps you may have felt a little insecure in the beginning yet now have learned that confidence ultimately comes from the Lord. You're beautiful, and God loves you.

FINAL THOUGHTS

Dear Lord, I pray over the next steps you have for the person reading this book. Perhaps they will re-read this devotional or share it with another. Maybe they will find another one that continues to bring them comfort and encouragement. Possibly they will write one of their own. Whatever the case may be, I pray that they are in the Word growing their relationship with you, remembering that nothing is too big for you, and that they may have many "Only God" moments throughout their lives.

REFERENCES

All Scripture quotations, unless otherwise indicated, are taken from the Holy Bible, English Standard Version, ESV

Hannah Brown, *God Bless This Mess: Learning to Live and Love Through Life's Best (and Worst) Moments* (New York: HarperCollins, 2021)

Cole & Savannah LaBrant, *Cole & Sav: Our Surprising Love Story* (Nashville: W Publishing Group, 2018)

Madison Prewett, *Made for This Moment: Standing Firm with Strength, Grace, and Courage* (Grand Rapids: Zondervan, 2021)

Madison Prewett Troutt, *The Love Everybody Wants: What You're Looking for Is Already Yours* (United States: WaterBrook, 2023)

Sophia Lucia and Ambry Mehr "The Sitch" podcast

Sadie Robertson "Woah That's Good" podcast

Terry Savelle Foy @terrysavellefoy on YouTube

Printed in the United States
by Baker & Taylor Publisher Services